Financial Math, Book 2
Contents

Introduction

Every day students encounter mathematics: purchasing food at restaurants and the grocery store, shopping for clothes, deciding how to spend their paycheck, comparing prices of cars. Whatever their situation, they need to have a basic understanding of how mathematics is used in business dealings. Understanding how math is used in business will help students make sound decisions about their personal finances.

Financial literacy is becoming increasingly important to educators who realize that students are graduating without basic knowledge of everyday financial matters. A strong foundation in personal finance education will enable young people to avoid financial mistakes that could have far-reaching consequences.

The *Financial Math* series helps bridge the gap between what students learn in traditional math classes and what they need to know for work and life.

Financial Math, Book 1 introduces students to some of the daily encounters they will have with mathematics. The book begins with a review of basic math to make sure students are comfortable with different types of numbers and how they are manipulated.

The book goes on to show how to use and interpret numbers as they relate to money and earnings. Once students have an understanding of how to work with money and how it is acquired, the book explores common activities such as shopping for items, comparing prices, interpreting sales prices, and making payments. The final chapter of this book addresses the need for insurance and the options available.

Financial Math, Book 2 picks up the discussion where *Book 1* ends by exploring more complex mathematical topics such as interest, bank accounts, and budgets.

This book contains several features that will help students learn and practice the topics presented. First, the book is organized into seven chapters that focus on a specific topic. Each chapter is further divided into individual lessons. Specific skills are explored within each lesson.

Features

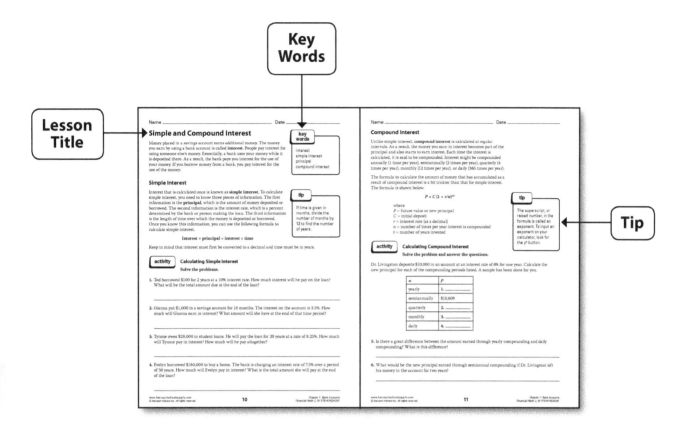

At the beginning of each lesson is a ***Key Words*** box. This box lists the important vocabulary words that appear in the lesson. These terms appear in boldface type within the lesson. They are described and defined in the lesson, and their definitions are listed in the Glossary at the end of the book.

In a ***Tip*** box, students will find information that will help them understand the content better or protect themselves when dealing with the concept in their daily life.

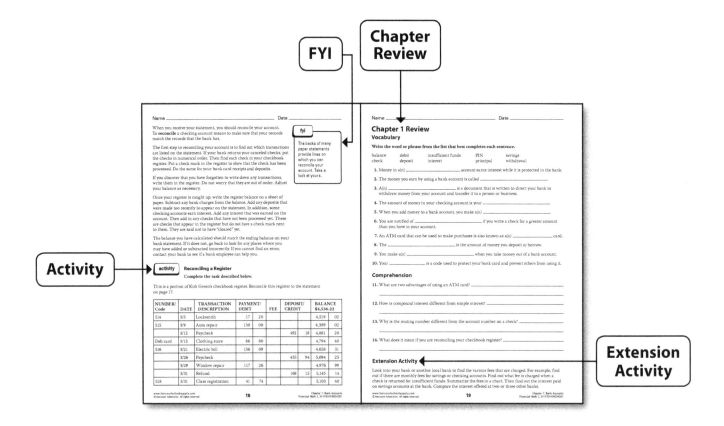

In an **FYI** box, students will find interesting information that relates to the topic.

Within each lesson, most often at the end of the lesson, is an ***Activity***. The activity is a task that gives students an opportunity to work with the concepts of the lesson and practice the skill presented.

At the end of each chapter is a ***Chapter Review*** of the topics presented throughout the entire chapter. The format of the Chapter Review will generally differ from the format of the lesson activities. The review will give students another opportunity to check that they understand the concepts within the lessons. Answers for the activities and the Chapter Reviews appear at the end of the book.

Each Chapter Review ends with an ***Extension Activity*** that challenges students to relate the concepts to their daily life in a hands-on way. It might involve looking at a pay stub, conducting research, or checking information in the local newspaper.

Assessment

Darken the circle for the correct answer.

1. Which form do you use to take money out of a savings account?

   Ⓐ deposit form

   Ⓑ withdrawal form

   Ⓒ 1040EZ

   Ⓓ W-2 form

2. Nicholas borrowed $500 for 2 years at a 10% interest rate. How much interest will he pay on the loan?

   Ⓐ $10   Ⓒ $100

   Ⓑ $50   Ⓓ $250

3. How many times a year does an account earn interest if it is compounded quarterly?

   Ⓐ once

   Ⓑ twice

   Ⓒ four times

   Ⓓ twelve times

4. A check shows sixty-eight dollars and $\frac{12}{100}$. What is this amount in numerals?

   Ⓐ $6.812   Ⓒ $682.00

   Ⓑ $68.12   Ⓓ $6,812.00

5. What does it mean if a check is returned to you for insufficient funds?

   Ⓐ You did not have enough money in your checking account.

   Ⓑ You wrote the checks out of numerical order.

   Ⓒ The check has been cashed and processed.

   Ⓓ You forgot to sign your name on the check.

6. Your check register shows a balance of $854.32. You write a check for $40.00 and withdraw $20 at the ATM. What is the new balance of your account?

   Ⓐ $794.32   Ⓒ $834.32

   Ⓑ $814.32   Ⓓ $914.32

7. What do you do when you reconcile your checkbook register?

   Ⓐ erase it

   Ⓑ shred it

   Ⓒ start it

   Ⓓ match it to bank records

8. If the APR on your credit card is 18%, what percentage do you pay each month on an outstanding balance?

   Ⓐ 1.5%   Ⓒ 12%

   Ⓑ 6%   Ⓓ 18%

9. All of the following will raise your credit score except

   Ⓐ paying your bills on time.

   Ⓑ paying your credit card balance each month.

   Ⓒ keeping your debt low.

   Ⓓ filing for bankruptcy.

10. You sign a lease that states you must pay $450 each month for two years. What is the total amount of rent you will pay during the life of the lease?

    Ⓐ $450   Ⓒ $5,400

    Ⓑ $4,500   Ⓓ $10,800

11. A buyer pays a down payment that is equal to 20% of the sale price of a home. If the home sells for $190,000, what is the amount of the down payment?

ⓐ $20,000   ⓒ $70,000

ⓑ $38,000   ⓓ $100,000

12. What would be the fee for a buyer to purchase 2 discount points on a home with a sale price of $275,000?

ⓐ $550   ⓒ $5,500

ⓑ $2,750   ⓓ $10,000

13. An appliance uses 250 kWh of electricity per month. If the electric company charges 7.15 cents per kWh, how much does it cost to use the appliance for a month?

ⓐ $1.79   ⓒ $178.75

ⓑ $17.88   ⓓ $250.00

14. A share that gives an individual ownership in part of a company is called a

ⓐ stock.   ⓒ CD.

ⓑ bond.   ⓓ IRA.

15. A savings account that is similar to a regular savings account but pays a higher interest rate, requires a higher minimum balance, and limits the number of withdrawals each month is a

ⓐ pension.

ⓑ individual retirement account.

ⓒ certificate of deposit.

ⓓ money market account.

16. Upon what does your standard deduction depend?

ⓐ number of dependents

ⓑ age and filing status

ⓒ state in which you live

ⓓ gross income

17. On which tax form do you list your charitable contributions?

ⓐ W-2   ⓒ W-4

ⓑ 1040EZ   ⓓ 1040 Schedule A

18. What does it mean to say that a leased car has a residual value?

ⓐ It is the total price of lease payments.

ⓑ It is the value at the end of the lease.

ⓒ It is the cost to insure the car.

ⓓ It is the purchase price plus interest payments.

19. Randi drives an average of 350 miles per week. Her car gets 24 miles to the gallon. If gas costs an average of $2.20 per gallon, about how much can Randi expect to spend on gasoline each month?

ⓐ $53   ⓒ $128

ⓑ $64   ⓓ $160

20. Jackson finds that his total assets add up to $124,690 and his total liabilities add to $96,800. What is his net worth?

ⓐ +$27,890   ⓒ +$221,490

ⓑ −$27,890   ⓓ −$221,490

Savings Account

You are earning enough money to start saving. You decide to open a savings account. A **savings account** is a bank account that earns money while protecting the money.

Deposits

You can add money to a savings account by making a **deposit**. One way to make a deposit is by completing a deposit form. You will usually receive deposit forms with your name and account number printed on them shortly after opening a savings account.

Another way to make a deposit is to make an arrangement with your employer. If you provide your employer with your account number and the routing number of the bank, your employer can deposit your paychecks directly into your account. This is known as **direct deposit**.

tip

In addition to your name, you will need your social security number, address, and telephone number to open a bank account. If you are a woman, you may also need your maiden name, which is your family name before you were married. You will generally need two forms of identification, one of which must have a photo on it.

activity

Using a Savings Deposit Form

Susie Saver has completed the deposit form below. Review the form and answer the questions.

				CASH			5	6		1	2
Susie Saver						1	4	4		9	8
Anywhere USA				C							
				H							
SAVINGS	DATE	3-15-08		E							
DEPOSIT				C							
				K							
				S							
Local Savings Bank				TOTAL $					.		

⑂⑃⑁⑆⑆⑁⑂⑁⑇⑂ ⑂⑁⑃⑈⑆⑁⑁⑂⑁

1. What is the name of Susie's bank? _____

2. How much did Susie deposit in cash? _____

3. How much did Susie deposit as a check? _____

4. What is Susie's account number? _____

5. Susie forgot to write the total amount of her deposit. What amount should she write on the form?

_____

Withdrawals

You can take money out of a savings account when you need it by
making a **withdrawal**. You can complete a withdrawal form that
tells the bank to take a certain amount of money out of your account.
A withdrawal form is very similar to a deposit form. It includes the
name of the bank, your name, the date, your account number, and
the amount you would like to withdraw.

fyi

The number to the
left of your account
number is the bank's
routing number. Each
bank is identified by a
different routing
number.

activity   Using a Savings Withdrawal Form

Review the withdrawal form below and answer the questions.

```
Wally Withdrawer
Anywhere, USA
                              DATE ____4-15-08____

SAVINGS
WITHDRAWAL        I WISH TO WITHDRAW FROM
                  MY SAVINGS ACCOUNT        $ [   ][ 9 ][ 3 ] . [ 5 ][ 0 ]


Working Bank

46815١242: 8١72١2
```

1. On what date was this form completed? _____

2. What was the amount of the withdrawal in words? _____

3. From which account number was the money withdrawn? _____

4. What is the name of the bank that maintains the account? _____

5. What is the routing number for the bank? _____

ATM and Debit Cards

In addition to using deposit and withdrawal forms, you can often access your account using an ATM card. **ATM** stands for *a*utomatic *t*eller *m*achine. An ATM card is a plastic card that looks much like a credit card. Using an ATM card, you can do most of the same things you can do at a bank even when the bank is closed or you are not near a bank branch. You can get cash, deposit money, check account balances, and withdraw funds using a personal identification number, or **PIN**, that you establish when you set up the account.

Some ATM cards, known as **debit cards**, can also be used to make purchases. When you use a debit card to buy something, you are asked to punch your PIN into a device. This enables the store to contact your bank electronically. The amount of the purchase is then deducted from your account and transferred to the store's account. The amount you can spend is limited by the amount in your bank account rather than any amount specified by the bank. However, most banks establish daily limits to the amount that may be withdrawn at an ATM.

Perhaps you have been in a store when you overheard a customer being asked "Debit or credit?" after handing a card to a cashier. The reason is that some ATM cards can be used in different ways. If they are used as debit, the funds are withdrawn immediately. If they are used as credit, the funds may take two or three business days to be transferred.

When a card is used as debit, many stores allow you to request additional cash when making a purchase. Suppose, for example, you purchase $56.78 worth of food at a local grocery store. You then request $20 cash back. A total of $76.78 will be withdrawn from your bank account. You will receive your groceries plus a $20 bill.

Be careful. A bank may charge a fee for using an ATM card. Most banks will allow you to use ATMs at their bank locations for free, but charge one or two dollars for using an ATM at another bank.

> **key words**
>
> ATM
> PIN
> debit card

> **tip**
>
> If you use ATMs frequently, fees can add up quickly. Avoid fees by using your own bank's ATMs or requesting extra cash when making purchases.

---

activity **Using ATM Cards**

Answer the questions.

1. Maya spent $43.26 at a store. She paid with a debit card and requested $25 cash back. What is the total amount that will be deducted from her bank account?

   _____

2. Last Saturday Theodore withdrew $50 at another bank's ATM. There is a fee of $2 for such a transaction. He then used his ATM card to purchase $36.12 worth of supplies for a home improvement project. What was the total amount that was deducted from his bank account that day?

   _____

Name _____   Date _____

Simple and Compound Interest

Money placed in a savings account earns additional money. The money you earn by using a bank account is called **interest**. People pay interest for using someone else's money. Essentially, a bank uses your money while it is deposited there. As a result, the bank pays you interest for the use of your money. If you borrow money from a bank, you pay interest for the use of the money.

key words

interest
simple interest
principal
compound interest

Simple Interest

Interest that is calculated once is known as **simple interest**. To calculate simple interest, you need to know three pieces of information. The first information is the **principal**, which is the amount of money deposited or borrowed. The second information is the interest rate, which is a percent determined by the bank or person making the loan. The third information is the length of time over which the money is deposited or borrowed. Once you know this information, you can use the following formula to calculate simple interest.

tip

If time is given in months, divide the number of months by 12 to find the number of years.

$$\textbf{Interest} = \textbf{principal} \times \textbf{interest} \times \textbf{time}$$

Keep in mind that interest must first be converted to a decimal and time must be in years.

activity **Calculating Simple Interest**

Solve the problems.

1. Ted borrowed $100 for 2 years at a 10% interest rate. How much interest will he pay on the loan? What will be the total amount due at the end of the loan?

_____

2. Gianna put $1,000 in a savings account for 18 months. The interest on the account is 3.5%. How much will Gianna earn in interest? What amount will she have at the end of that time period?

_____

3. Tyrone owes $28,000 in student loans. He will pay the loan for 20 years at a rate of 8.25%. How much will Tyrone pay in interest? How much will he pay altogether?

_____

4. Evelyn borrowed $180,000 to buy a home. The bank is charging an interest rate of 7.5% over a period of 30 years. How much will Evelyn pay in interest? What is the total amount she will pay at the end of the loan?

_____

Compound Interest

Unlike simple interest, **compound interest** is calculated at regular intervals. As a result, the money you earn in interest becomes part of the principal and also starts to earn interest. Each time the interest is calculated, it is said to be compounded. Interest might be compounded annually (1 time per year), semiannually (2 times per year), quarterly (4 times per year), monthly (12 times per year), or daily (365 times per year).

The formula to calculate the amount of money that has accumulated as a result of compound interest is a bit trickier than that for simple interest. The formula is shown below.

$$P = C (1 + r/n)^{nt}$$

where
P = future value or new principal
C = initial deposit
r = interest rate (as a decimal)
n = number of times per year interest is compounded
t = number of years invested

tip

The superscript, or raised number, in the formula is called an exponent. To input an exponent on your calculator, look for the y^x button.

activity   **Calculating Compound Interest**

Solve the problem and answer the questions.

Dr. Livingston deposits $10,000 in an account at an interest rate of 6% for one year. Calculate the new principal for each of the compounding periods listed. A sample has been done for you.

n	P
yearly	1. _____
semiannually	$10,609
quarterly	2. _____
monthly	3. _____
daily	4. _____

5. Is there a great difference between the amount earned through yearly compounding and daily compounding? What is this difference?

_____

6. What would be the new principal earned through semiannual compounding if Dr. Livingston left his money in the account for two years?

_____

Checking Accounts

There are many payments for which you will be unable to use cash or debit cards. You will often need to pay bills using a checking account. A **checking account** is a bank account into which you deposit money that you can spend using checks instead of cash.

A **check** is a document that you give to a person or business you want to pay. That person then brings your check to a bank. Information on the check tells your bank to take money out of your checking account and transfer it to that person or business.

Writing information on a check properly is essential to making sure your bank transfers the correct amount of money. Mistakes on a check can cause the check to be returned to you, or it can cause the bank to take out a different amount of money than you had intended. For this reason, you should follow several basic steps every time you write a check. Keep in mind that the specific details of a check can vary from bank to bank, but all checks have the same basic format.

Step 1: Write the date. You can write the date in any format as long as it is clear. Include the month, the day, and the year.

Step 2: Write the name of the person or company receiving your check. The check will have a line on which to write this information. Before the line, you will find the words *Pay to the order of* or *Payable to.* Be sure to use full names rather than nicknames and abbreviations unless otherwise indicated.

Step 3: Write the dollar amount in the box that begins with a dollar sign ($). Write the amount as a decimal number with dollars and cents. For example, $32.18. Try not to leave any blank space in the box. If there is extra space, simply draw a line through it. This prevents someone else from adding numbers to your amount.

---

key words

checking account
check

---

tip

Always use blue or black ink to write a check. Never use pencil, and avoid other colors of ink.

Step 4: Write the amount of the check using words for the dollar part and a fraction for the cents. The bottom of the fraction is always 100 because there are 100 cents in a dollar.

Separate dollars and cents with the word *and*. For example, thirty-two and 18/100. Once you have done this, draw a straight line to fill up the remaining space. This prevents anything else from being written on the line to change the amount.

Step 5: Most checks have a line at the lower left that has the words *Memo* or *For*. You can use this line to write what the check is for. You can fill this in or leave it blank. It is not required by the bank.

Step 6: Sign your name on the line in the lower right part of the check. You cannot print your name. You must sign in script or cursive writing. Include your first name, last name, and middle initial if you use one. A check is not valid unless you sign it. You should try to sign your name in the same general way every time.

tip

Never sign a check unless you have filled in all the information.

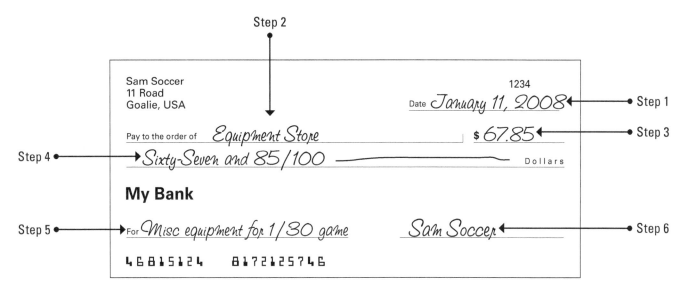

Name _____ Date _____

 Writing a Check

Complete the following task.

Susie Student needs to pay $48.26 to Zappy Electric Company and $173.89 to Reliable Car Leasing. Pretend that you are Susie Student. Fill out the two blank checks to pay these bills.

Susie Student
Class Court
Anywhere, USA

106

Date _____

Pay to the order of _____ $ _____

_____ D o l l a r s

Local Savings Bank

For _____   _____

⑈⑈⑆⑂⑈⑈⑄⑆   ⑆⑈⑈⑂⑄⑄⑆⑆⑂⑈

Susie Student
Class Court
Anywhere, USA

107

Date _____

Pay to the order of _____ $ _____

_____ D o l l a r s

Local Savings Bank

For _____   _____

⑈⑈⑆⑂⑈⑈⑄⑆   ⑆⑈⑈⑂⑄⑄⑆⑆⑂⑈

Chapter 1: Bank Accounts
Financial Math 2, SV 9781419034381

Name _____   Date _____

Using a Bank Account Register

Each time you make a deposit or withdraw money from a bank account, the amount of money in your account changes. You need to keep track of any changes to your account. This is of particular importance for a checking account. You cannot write checks adding up to more money than is in your account. If you do, your check will be returned to you for **insufficient funds**.

You may have heard the term *bounce*. When there is not enough money in a checking account to pay a check, the check is said to bounce. You are then charged a fee for writing the check. The person who received the check is also charged a fee.

To avoid fees for returned checks, you need to keep track of the checks you write. Your checkbook comes with a **register**, which is a table you can use to calculate the amount of money in your checking account.

At the top right-hand part of the register, you write the starting balance for your account. Your **balance** is the amount of money in your checking account at a given time. If you take money out of or put money into your account, you must change the balance.

tip

Don't write future dates on a check, known as postdating, if you don't have the funds at the time. If the check is cashed early, it will bounce.

NUMBER/ Code	DATE	TRANSACTION DESCRIPTION	PAYMENT/ DEBIT		FEE	DEPOSIT/ CREDIT		BALANCE $1,295.82	
189	11/5	Water Company	84	69				1,211	13
Deposit	11/6	Cash Deposit				50	00	1,261	13
Debit	11/6	Flower Shop	23	46				1,237	67
190	11/8	Lawn Company	45	00				1,192	67

activity   Reading a Register

Answer the questions.

1. What is the starting balance? _____

2. What is the balance on 11/8? _____

3. What is the total amount of deposits shown? _____

4. What is the total amount of withdrawals shown? _____

Although registers differ, you generally write the number of the check in the first column. You may also note if you made a withdrawal, a deposit, or a purchase with a debit card. Some registers have separate columns for this information.

Next to the check number, write the date on which you made the transaction. Space is limited, so writing the month/day is usually enough.

The next column is where you describe the transaction. For example, you might write the name of the person or company you wrote the check to or the source of the money for a deposit.

tip

Write only one transaction on each line in the register.

In the *Payment/Debit* column, write any amount removed from the account. It might be by check, withdrawal, or ATM card. Show the exact payment, including dollars and cents. Once you have written the amount, subtract it from the existing balance. Write the new amount in the column labeled *Balance*.

Write any deposits you make in the *Deposit/Credit* column. Once you have written the amount, add it to the existing balance. Write the new amount in the column labeled *Balance*.

activity   **Completing a Register**

Complete the tasks.

Patrick made the following transactions. Enter each one into the register on page 15.

11/10   Wrote check 191 for $24.30 to Current News Co.

11/11   Used a debit card to purchase $68.51 in groceries at All About Food.

11/14   Paycheck for $892.78 from Quick Delivery Service was direct deposited into account.

11/15   Wrote check 192 for $252.25 to Speedy Cars for car payment.

What is Patrick's ending balance after all of the transactions? _____

Name _____ Date _____

Reconciling a Checkbook Register

Once a month you will receive a statement from your bank. You may also be able to access your statement online if you set up this feature with your account. The statement shows any changes to your account during the statement period. This includes checks you have written, withdrawals you have made at an ATM, purchases you have made using a debit card, and any deposits you have made. It also shows any fees you may have been charged.

Local Savings Bank   # MONTHLY STATEMENT

Kirk Green   Ending Date: 3/31/08
52 Savings Way   Account: 8921463
Anywhere, USA

Previous Balance	$4,536.22
2 Deposits and Credits	$ 928.12
6 Checks and Debits	$ 543.76
Current Balance	$4,920.58

DEPOSITS AND CREDITS

DATE	AMOUNT	DESCRIPTION
3-12	$492.18	Deposit
3-26	$435.94	Deposit

CHECKS AND DEBITS

DATE	NUMBER/DESCRIPTION	AMOUNT
3-5	514	17.20
3-9	515	130.00
3-15	Purchase	86.80
3-21	516	136.09
3-24	517	56.41
3-29	Purchase	117.26

Financial Math 2, SV 9781419034381

When you receive your statement, you should reconcile your account. To **reconcile** a checking account means to make sure that your records match the records that the bank has.

The first step to reconciling your account is to find out which transactions are listed on the statement. If your bank returns your canceled checks, put the checks in numerical order. Then find each check in your checkbook register. Put a check mark in the register to show that the check has been processed. Do the same for your bank card receipts and deposits.

If you discover that you have forgotten to write down any transactions, write them in the register. Do not worry that they are out of order. Adjust your balance as necessary.

Once your register is caught up, write the register balance on a sheet of paper. Subtract any bank charges from the balance. Add any deposits that were made too recently to appear on the statement. In addition, some checking accounts earn interest. Add any interest that was earned on the account. Then add in any checks that have not been processed yet. These are checks that appear in the register but do not have a check mark next to them. They are said not to have "cleared" yet.

The balance you have calculated should match the ending balance on your bank statement. If it does not, go back to look for any places where you may have added or subtracted incorrectly. If you cannot find an error, contact your bank to see if a bank employee can help you.

> **fyi**
>
> The backs of many paper statements provide lines on which you can reconcile your account. Take a look at yours.

activity   Reconciling a Register

Complete the task described below.

This is a portion of Kirk Green's checkbook register. Reconcile this register to the statement on page 17.

NUMBER/ Code	DATE	TRANSACTION DESCRIPTION	PAYMENT/ DEBIT		FEE	DEPOSIT/ CREDIT		BALANCE $4,536.22	
514	3/5	Locksmith	17	20				4,519	02
515	3/9	Auto repair	130	00				4,389	02
	3/12	Paycheck				492	18	4,881	20
Deb card	3/15	Clothing store	86	80				4,794	40
516	3/21	Electric bill	136	09				4,658	31
	3/26	Paycheck				435	94	5,094	25
	3/29	Window repair	117	26				4,976	99
	3/31	Refund				168	15	5,145	14
518	3/31	Class registration	41	74				5,103	40

Chapter 1 Review

Vocabulary

Write the word or phrase from the list that best completes each sentence.

balance	debit	insufficient funds	PIN	savings
check	deposit	interest	principal	withdrawal

1. Money in a(n) _____ account earns interest while it is protected in the bank.

2. The money you earn by using a bank account is called _____.

3. A(n) _____ is a document that is written to direct your bank to withdraw money from your account and transfer it to a person or business.

4. The amount of money in your checking account is your _____.

5. When you add money to a bank account, you make a(n) _____.

6. You are notified of _____ if you write a check for a greater amount than you have in your account.

7. An ATM card that can be used to make purchases is also known as a(n) _____ card.

8. The _____ is the amount of money you deposit or borrow.

9. You make a(n) _____ when you take money out of a bank account.

10. Your _____ is a code used to protect your bank card and prevent others from using it.

Comprehension

11. What are two advantages of using an ATM card? _____

_____

12. How is compound interest different from simple interest? _____

_____

13. Why is the routing number different from the account number on a check? _____

_____

14. What does it mean if you are reconciling your checkbook register? _____

_____

Extension Activity

Look into your bank or another local bank to find the various fees that are charged. For example, find out if there are monthly fees for savings or checking accounts. Find out what fee is charged when a check is returned for insufficient funds. Summarize the fees in a chart. Then find out the interest paid on savings accounts at the bank. Compare the interest offered at two or three other banks.

Credit Cards

They are all around you. Most people have at least one. Some have many. They are credit cards. A **credit card** allows you to pay for merchandise or services by borrowing against a line of credit. You then make monthly payments on the outstanding balance.

For example, suppose a bank offers you a credit card with a line of credit of $10,000. That means that you can purchase up to $10,000 of merchandise or services. Rather than being withdrawn immediately from your bank account as would occur with a debit card, the amount is essentially lent to you by the credit card company.

Each month, you will receive a bill from the credit card company. You have the option to pay the entire amount. However, you may also make a minimum payment. The **minimum payment** is the lowest amount that you are required to pay on your credit card debt.

A credit card company may allow you a grace period. The **grace period** is the length of time from when you make a purchase to when the company begins charging you interest on that purchase. If there is not a grace period, interest will start accumulating immediately.

After the grace period ends, the credit card company begins charging interest on your balance. The interest you pay on the money you owe to the credit card company is known as the **finance charge**. Many companies compute a monthly finance charge based on your average daily balance for the month and charge interest on that amount. Others calculate finance charges on the average daily balance plus any new purchases.

This finance charge is expressed as an **annual percentage rate (APR)**. The APR is often between 10% and 21%. An APR of 18%, for example, does not mean you are paying 18% every month. It is what you would pay over the course of a year. Instead, you would pay $\frac{1}{12}$ of 18%, or 1.5%, every month.

You should compare the APR for different credit cards before selecting one. Some credit card companies may offer an introductory rate. An introductory rate is a temporary, lower APR that usually lasts for 6 months before converting to a normal rate. Make sure you know when the introductory rate ends so you are not fooled into thinking the APR is lower than it truly is.

> **key words**
>
> credit card
> minimum payment
> grace period
> finance charge
> annual percentage
>   rate (APR)

> **fyi**
>
> You should look for a card with a grace period of 25 days or more and try to pay off the balance before that period ends. You avoid finance charges if you pay your entire balance at once.

activity | Computing Finance Charges and Fees

Situation A

1. A credit card company uses your average daily balance to compute your finance charge. You charge $100 on May 2 and $200 on May 20. What is your average daily balance?

2. If the APR on this credit card is 18%, what would the finance charge be for May?

Situation B

3. A credit card company uses the outstanding balance at the beginning of the billing cycle to compute the finance charge. As of February 1, which is the beginning of the billing cycle, you have a credit card balance of $5,000. On February 5, you pay off the entire balance and do not use the card again during the month. What will the finance charge be when you receive your bill at the end of the billing cycle if you are charged an APR of 12%?

Situation C

4. In addition to interest, a credit card company charges a transaction fee of 2.5% of the amount. If you take a cash advance of $3,000, what transaction fee will you pay?

Situation D

5. You have a credit card balance of $500 due on August 18. You send a check for $250, but your check does not arrive until August 20. The bank charges a late fee of $35. You do not add any additional charges to the card, and the company uses your average daily balance to compute your finance charge. If the APR is 20%, what will be the total charges on the next bill?

Credit Reports and Credit Applications

Your credit report determines whether you receive a credit card, as well as the APR you are given should you qualify for credit. A **credit report** is a summary of your financial history that indicates if you pay your bills on time, how much money you have in your bank accounts, and how much money you owe.

At present, there are three major companies that maintain credit reports: Equifax, Experian, and TransUnion. These companies, otherwise known as credit bureaus, collect financial information and organize it into a report that can be made available to people and agencies from which you may want credit.

A typical credit report includes the following information:

- Your name and social security number
- Your current and previous addresses
- Information about your current and past loans
- Your public record information (bankruptcies, court judgments, liens)
- A list of companies that have reviewed your credit
- Your payment history
- The length of your credit history
- Your current and previous employers

Potential lenders look at your credit report to find out how you handle debt. It helps them decide if you are a good candidate to lend money to and whether they will get their money back. A good credit report can be very helpful in life when you want to finance a car, a home, or an education. Not only will it help you obtain a loan, but it will help you to secure a lower interest rate.

A bad credit report can cause you many problems by preventing lenders from working with you. Even if you do obtain a loan or credit card, you will likely pay higher interest rates than if you had a good credit report.

Another problem can be lack of credit. The best way to develop credit is to apply for a credit card. Once you have one, use it wisely and pay off your balance in full each month. Over time, you will establish yourself as someone who can handle debt and repay loans.

> **key words**
>
> credit report
> credit score

> **tip**
>
> You should check your credit report regularly for any mistakes. The Fair Credit Reporting Act (FCRA) entitles you to a free annual credit report. The three nationwide consumer reporting companies mentioned on this page will provide free annual credit reports only through annualcreditreport. com, 1-877-322-8228, and Annual Credit Report Request Service, P.O. Box 105281, Atlanta, GA 30348-5281.

A credit report is summarized by a credit score. A **credit score** is a number that represents a measure of your credit risk. It is calculated through a complex mathematical formula that takes various aspects of your credit history into account. The credit score gives lenders a way to compare you with other consumers and to calculate the interest rate at which you may borrow money.

Credit scores range from 300 to 900. To get the most favorable interest rates, you'll need a credit score of 720 or higher. On average, a person with a credit score of 520 will get interest rates on loans that are three to four percentage points higher than a person with a score of 720.

Your credit report and score are very important information. Not just anyone can gain access to this information. The Fair Credit Reporting Act (FCRA) specifies who can access your credit report and why. According to the FCRA, a company must have a legitimate reason to view your credit report. Any organization or individual who obtains a copy of your credit report under false pretenses can be fined and jailed for up to a year.

The types of companies that can access your credit report include lenders, insurance companies, landlords, potential employers, and government child support agencies. Keep in mind that any time your credit report is viewed, it is reported on your credit report. The more report inquiries that show up on the report, the lower your credit score becomes.

activity — Reading a Credit Report

Study the credit report on page 24 and answer the questions below.

1. What is the name of the individual described in the report? _____

2. On what date was the credit report prepared? _____

3. Which of the credit card accounts has been closed? _____

4. What amount was turned over to Pro Collections Agency? _____

5. When did the individual file bankruptcy? _____

6. What organizations requested a credit report in 2003? _____

7. Why was the individual's checking account closed in 2002? _____

Name _____ Date _____

John Doe
123 Home Address
City, State 00000

Date 03/04/08
Social Security Number 123-45-6789
Date of Birth 04/19/57

Please address all future
correspondence to the
address on the right:

Credit Reporting Office
Business Address
City, State 00000

CREDIT HISTORY

Company Name	Account Number	Whose Account	Date Opened	Months Re-viewed	Date of Last Activity	*High Credit	Terms	Items as of Date Reported			Date Reported
								Balance	Past Due	Status	
Sears	1125151	J	05/86	66	12/03	3500	0	0		R1	02/04
Citibank	2953900 0001004	I	11/86	48	11/03	9388	48M	0		11	12/03
AMEX	3554112 51511	A	06/87	24	10/02	500		0 Closed Account		O1	12/03
Chase	5422977	I	05/85	48	01/04	5000	340	3000	680	R3	

*Amount in H/C Column is Credit Limit

**************************PRIOR PAYING HISTORY**********************************
>>>30(03) 60(04) 90+(01) 08/02-R2,   02/02-R3,   10/01-R4<<<<

**************************COLLECTION ACCOUNTS***********************************
>>>Collection Reported 06/00; Assigned 09/99 TO PRO COLL(800) 555-1234 Client – ABC Hospital, Amount - $978;
Stat Unpaid –6/00; Balance-$978 06/00 Date of Last Activity 09/99; Individual; Account Number 787652JC

>>>>>>>>>>>>>>>>>>>>>>>>>COLLECTION AGENCY TELEPHONE NUMBER(S)<<<<<<<<<<<<<<<<<<<<<<<<
PRO COLL (800)555-1234

**************************COURTHOUSE RECORDS***********************************
>>>>Lien Filed 03/02; Fulton Cty; CASE NUMBER – 32114; AMOUNT - $26,667, Class – City/County; Released 07/02;
Verified 09/03

>>>>Bankruptcy Filed 12/99; Northern Dist Ct; Case Number 673HC12; Liabilities - $15,787; Personal Individual; Discharged;
Assets $780

>>>>Judgment Filed 12/99; Fulton Cty; Case Number 898872; Defendant – John Doe; Amount - $8,984; Plaintiff – ABC Real
Estate; Satisfied 03/02; Verified 05/03

**************************ADDITIONAL INFORMATION*******************************
Former Address 456 Jupiter Rd., Atlanta, GA 30245

Former Address P.O. Box 2138, Savannah, GA 31406

Last Reported Employment   Engineer, Space Patrol

Checking Account Opened 09/98
Closed 05/02 Reason: Insufficient funds
In the amount of $400

**********************COMPANIES THAT REQUESTED YOUR CREDIT HISTORY******************

03/04/04 EQUIFAX
12/16/03 PRM VISA
06/11/03 NATIONS BANK

02/12/04 MACYS
08/01/03 AM CITIBANK
04/29/03 GE CAPITAL

Name _____ Date _____

Taking Out a Loan

You want to buy a car, but you don't have enough money. What do you do? You might take out a loan. A **loan** is a sum of money lent to a borrower at a specified interest rate. When you accept a loan, you agree to pay it back over a set period of time. The amount of money you borrow is called the principal, and the interest is the cost of borrowing the money. The length of time determined for paying back the loan is known as the **term** of the loan.

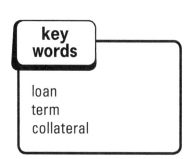

It is best to take out a loan only for a large expense, such as a car, college tuition, or a house. Taking out loans for smaller purchases or taking out many loans at once can cause financial and credit problems for you.

The interest rate on a loan is determined by the lender. In addition to interest, a lender may charge other fees such as an application fee or a fee to check your credit. These fees are often called points.

You can generally obtain a loan from a bank or credit union. The best way to compare loan offers is to look at the APR offered by each institution and the fees.

Installment Loan

One common type of loan is an installment loan. When you accept an installment loan, you borrow all of the money at once. You then repay the money in set amounts, called installments, on a regular schedule over a period of time.

Installment loan customers often make payments using a coupon book that has a slip for each payment. Each slip lists the date and the amount due. For some installment loans, the bank will send a reminder each month before the due date. The reminder usually lists information about the loan and has a portion that can be returned with payment.

activity   **Analyzing an Installment Loan**

Read the example and answer the questions.

Mr. Ramos borrows $5,000 at 8.2% for 5 years in order to make some improvements to his home.

1. What is the principal? _____

2. What is the interest rate? _____

3. What is the term of the loan? _____

Line of Credit

A line of credit is a type of revolving credit. It allows you to write checks for the amount you want to borrow up to a limit set by the lender. For example, you may receive a line of credit of $10,000. The credit does not cost anything until you write a check. Once you write a check, you begin to pay interest on the amount you borrowed. So, for example, if you write a check for $6,000, you will pay interest on that amount. You still have $4,000 available to borrow. If you then make a payment of $1,000, you have $5,000 available to borrow.

Types of Loans

There are many different types of loans to consider. Here is a brief review of some of them.

Unsecured Loan

You can obtain an unsecured loan solely on your promise to repay it. This type of loan is risky for the lender and usually involves a higher interest rate than other types of loans.

Secured Loan

When you obtain a secure loan, you must put up property as **collateral**. If you fail to repay the loan, the lender can take your collateral. Home equity loans are common types of secured loans. In this type of loan, an individual uses a home as collateral and borrows against the value of the home.

Fixed Rate Loan

When you obtain a fixed rate loan, the interest rate and monthly payments stay the same over the length of the loan.

Adjustable Rate Loan

If you obtain an adjustable rate loan, the interest rate can change. It usually changes with the federal interest rate. As a result, the monthly payments change as well. There is usually a limit on the change that can occur.

 Potential Line of Credit

Complete the following task.

A lender sets the credit limit on a home equity line of credit as 75% of the appraised value of a home minus the balance owed on the existing mortgage.

Suppose a homeowner has a home appraised at $200,000 with an existing mortgage balance of $95,000. What credit limit would the lender set for this individual?

Chapter 2 Review

Use the following words or phrases to complete the paragraph.

APR	credit score	line of credit
balance	finance charge	loan
collateral	grace period	minimum payment
credit card	installment	principal
credit report	interest	term

When you purchase an item without using cash, you might use your **(1.)** _____.

At the end of the 25-day **(2.)** _____, you will receive a statement. If you

make only the **(3.)** _____ instead of your entire **(4.)** _____, you will have

to pay a(n) **(5.)** _____ in addition to the cost of the item. If you need to purchase a large

item, such as a car, you may wish to apply for a(n) **(6.)** _____ at a bank. The bank

will request a copy of your **(7.)** _____. If the bank agrees to lend you money, it will

use a number called your **(8.)** _____ to determine your **(9.)** _____.

You might obtain a(n) **(10.)** _____ loan, for which you will pay fixed payments, or a(n)

(11.) _____, for which you will write checks as you need them. The bank will help you

determine the amount of the **(12.)** _____ you should request as well as the length, or

(13.) _____, of the loan.

Critical Thinking

14. Why might a person use a credit card even if he or she intends to pay off the entire balance within
the grace period?

_____

Completing a Form

15. The first step to obtaining credit is often to apply for a credit card. Part of a credit card application
appears on page 28. Fill in all the information so you can become familiar with the type of
information you might need to know.

Extension Activity

Obtain advertisements or brochures concerning loans from local banks. Identify and compare the APR
and fees associated with each loan.

Name _____ Date _____

CREDIT CARD APPLICATION

Name   First _____ M.I. _____ Last _____

Date of Birth   _____/_____/_____
                    MM/DD/YYYY

Social Security Number   _____/_____/_____

Street Address   City_____

State _____ ZIP_____

Housing Status   Years There _____

Housing Payment $_____.00 per month

Home Phone   (_____) _____-_____

Mother's Maiden Name   _____

Are you a U.S. citizen or permanent resident?   _____Yes _____No

E-mail Address   _____

STUDENT INFORMATION

Please complete this section if you are currently a student and ensure that all fields in the employment information section are left blank.

Student Status   _____ Full _____ Part _____ Recent Graduate _____ Not a Student

School Name   _____

Major   _____

Graduation Year   _____

Campus Telephone   (_____) _____-_____

Permanent Home Address   City_____

State _____ ZIP_____

Source of Personal Income   _____ Part-time Job _____ Full-time Job _____ Other

Total Personal Income $_____.00 per month

Employer   _____

Position   _____

Employment Status   _____

Chapter 2: Borrowing Money
Financial Math 2, SV 9781419034381

Types of Leases

You are ready to rent an apartment, condominium, or house. When you rent, you must sign a lease. A **lease** is a legal contract that defines a relationship between the owner, called the lessor, and the renter, called the lessee. The lessor is also known as the landlord and the lessee as the tenant. The lease describes all of the terms involved in the rental agreement, including the length of time a lessee may use it and what condition it must be in when returned to the landlord. The amount of the payments and any financial penalties for late payments or damage are also described in the lease.

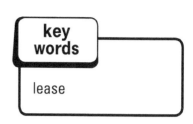

key words

lease

There are several different types of leases.

Fixed Lease

In this type of lease, the renter pays a fixed rental amount for the duration of the lease. So, for example, you might agree to pay $950 for rent every month for 13 months. Separately, you must pay all of the expenses related to the rental unit, such as utilities and insurance.

Gross Lease

In this type of lease, the renter pays a flat monthly amount. Out of this amount, the landlord must pay all operating costs for the unit. For example, you might pay a fee of $1,200 per month, but you do not pay related expenses, such as utilities and insurance, separately.

Net Lease

In this type of lease, the tenant agrees to pay, in addition to the rent, expenses such as taxes, insurance, maintenance, and other costs of the leased property. This type of lease is similar to a gross lease except the additional payments are based on actual costs rather than estimates.

Step Lease

In this type of lease, the rent is scheduled to increase by a set amount on an annual basis during the life of the agreement. The increase is planned to cover expected increases in the costs incurred by the lessor.

fyi

Many small businesses and retail stores sign leases for space.

Cost-of-Living Leases

In this type of lease, the rent is tied to the cost-of-living index. The rent goes up with general inflation.

Name _____ Date _____

Rental Deposit

When you sign a lease, you will usually be asked to pay a deposit known as a rental or security deposit. This is a fee that the landlord holds to pay for any damages incurred by the rental unit. If at the end of the lease the unit is in good condition as described by the lease, the deposit will be returned to you. If not, the landlord is entitled to withhold the portion of the deposit required to pay for repairs.

 Paying Rent

Complete the tasks below.

1. A lease states that you must pay a fixed rate of $1,000 per month along with a deposit equal to one month's rent. The lease extends for a period of 24 months. How much will you pay throughout the life of the lease? _____

2. A lease states that you must pay a fixed rate of $800 per month for the first year. At the end of the first year, the monthly payment will increase by 2.5%. How much will you pay during the first two years of this lease? _____

3. A lease states that you must pay a fixed rate of $11,700 per year paid in equal, monthly installments. In addition to rent, you can expect to pay $45 for electricity, $30 for water, and $60 for insurance each month. How much can you expect to pay on a monthly basis for rent, electricity, water, and insurance? _____

4. A gross lease states that you must pay a fixed monthly rate of $1,200 plus a deposit of $950. How much will you pay to rent this unit for one year? _____

Affording Rent

A common rule states that your annual rent should be no more than 30% of your annual income. To decide if you can afford a rental unit, divide the annual rent by 0.30. This calculates the amount you need to earn annually so that rent is no more than 30% of your income.

 Affording Rent

Complete the tasks below.

5. You want to rent a one-bedroom apartment that costs $700 per month. How much would you have to earn in a year for this to be no more than 30% of your income?

_____

6. You earn an annual salary of $38,000. What is the greatest amount of monthly rent you can afford if you do not want to pay more than 30% of your annual income?

_____

Name _____ Date _____

Renters' Rights and Responsibilities

A lease is a legally binding contract. Both the lessor and the lessee have rights and responsibilities as a result of that contract. The specific rights and responsibilities are stipulated by the laws of each state. There are basic items that most states have in common.

Renters' Rights

- Some or all of an application fee must be returned if the application is denied.

- The renter's personal information must be protected by the landlord and can be released only under certain situations, such as if the landlord has written permission or is involved in a legal case relating to the lessee and the rental unit.

- The landlord must provide the renter with a report of any damage in the unit within days of occupancy.

- The renter must be informed of any change in management, ownership, or other use of the property within a specific period of time, such as six months.

- The renter is entitled to live in a safe place that meets local building and health codes. The renter has the right to a safe environment, which may involve locks and notice prior to the spraying of pesticides and other chemicals.

- The renter is guaranteed the rent stated in the lease until the end of the contract. Written notice must be provided of any rent increases prior to the expiration of the contract.

- A landlord cannot ask a renter for a deposit that is greater than an amount equal to two months' rent. The deposit must be returned within a specified period after the renter vacates the unit. If there are any deductions, the landlord must supply a written list of damages and charges.

Renters' Responsibilities

- The renter must be truthful in all information provided on the rental application.
- The renter must pay the rent on time without having to be reminded by the landlord.
- The renter must follow the terms of the lease.
- The renter must keep the rental unit in good condition, obeying safety and health codes.
- The renter must give the landlord a written notice in advance of the time he or she is moving out. The amount of time is usually stipulated in the lease.

activity — Reading a Lease Agreement

Answer the questions below after reading the portion of the lease agreement on page 33.

1. On what day was the lease signed? _____

2. Who is the renter? _____

3. By what date is the rent due each month? _____

4. What is the amount of the monthly rent? _____

5. What fee must the renter pay if the rent is late? _____

6. Who will pay the electricity bill each month? _____

7. Who will pay the trash bill each month? _____

8. What is the amount of the security deposit collected? _____

9. On what day can the renter move into the unit? _____

10. What is the length of the lease? _____

11. Who is the landlord? _____

12. On what date does the lease end? _____

13. What form of payment must the tenant use to pay the rent? _____

14. Other than electricity, what utilities does the tenant pay? _____

15. How much pet deposit will the renter pay? _____

Name _____ Date _____

LEASE AGREEMENT

This agreement is made on May 15, 2008 between

_____ J and L Enterprises _____ (**landlord**), _____ Rita Renter _____ (**tenant**)

address: _____ 60 Business Way _____ address: _____ 9876 Town Way _____

_____ Corporation, CA 33333 _____ _____ City, CA 55555 _____

phone: _____ 888-910-9000 _____ phone: _____ 888-222-2000 _____

I. Terms of Agreement Summary

Address of property to be leased: _____ 1234 Apartment Avenue   Condo, CA 44444 _____

Lease term begins: _____ June 1, 2008 _____ ends: _____ May 31, 2009 _____

Length of term: _____ 12 _____ (months)

Total rent payment for full term: _____ $13,200 _____

Monthly payment: _____ $1,100 _____

Payment is due on the _____ 5th day _____ of each month.

Payment accepted includes: X check __credit card __cash

In the event that monthly payments are not made by the designated date, a late charge will be assessed of $ _____ 10 _____ per _____ day _____ (length of time).

Utilities shall be paid as followed:

	LANDLORD	TENANT
Electricity:		X
Gas:		X
Water:		X
Trash:	X	
Heat:		X
Other:		

Monies received from Tenant(s) as follows:

Security Deposit (deposited with Landlord/Agent)	$1,100
Pet Deposit of	NA
First Month's Rent	$1,100
Pro-rated Rent	NA
Pet Rent (if applicable)	NA
Other Charges: specify:	
TOTAL:	

Renter's Insurance

Even though you don't own the place where you live, you still want to protect your possessions inside it. To accomplish this, you can purchase renter's insurance. **Renter's insurance** is a policy that can protect your personal property against fire, theft, or vandalism. It could also protect you in the case of a liability lawsuit against you. This might happen, for example, if someone is injured while visiting you.

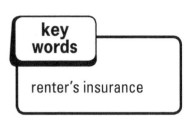

key words

renter's insurance

There are several items to consider when purchasing a renter's insurance policy.

Dollar Amount of Coverage

A fixed amount is determined for all of your possessions. The price of the policy is related to this amount.

Deductible

The deductible is the amount that you must pay before your insurance benefit is paid.

Actual Cash Value (ACV) or Replacement Cost

This determines how much you are reimbursed when your property is damaged or destroyed. Suppose your television is broken during a lightning storm. An ACV policy will pay you the value of the property at the time of the loss. If you had bought the television several years prior to the incident and it was not in the greatest shape, you will not receive a large sum for your loss. A replacement cost policy will pay the amount required to replace the television. In this case, it will pay the cost of purchasing a new television that is similar to the television you bought originally.

activity   **Comparing Renter's Insurance**
Complete the task below.

Renter A has an ACV renter's policy that costs $140 annually. Renter B has a replacement cost policy that costs $180 annually. During a storm, the roof over their apartments is damaged. Leaking water damages both of their stereo systems. They have identical stereo systems that cost $500 four years ago. The current value of the stereo system is $125. The cost to buy a new stereo system that is comparable to the original is $625. Consider the cost of the insurance policy, the benefit paid, and the cost to replace the stereo. Which renter paid a lower total to get a new stereo as a result of the storm?

Costs of Buying a Home

An individual has been renting a home for several years and wants to purchase a home. The biggest hurdle to purchasing a home is often acquiring a down payment. A **down payment** is an amount you pay when you acquire a house. It is the difference between the price of the home and the loan, which is known as a **mortgage**.

Lenders traditionally require the down payment to be 20% of the home's purchase price. That means if the purchase price of the home is $250,000, the down payment would be $50,000.

Many lenders will accept less than 20% of the home's purchase if the borrower takes out private mortgage insurance (PMI). Private mortgage insurance protects a lender in the event that a borrower does not pay, or defaults, on the loan. Essentially, the borrower pays the premium, but the lender receives the protection.

The annual cost of PMI varies from 0.19% to 0.9% of the total loan value. The actual percentage depends on the loan term, loan type, and portion of the total home value that is financed.

> **key words**
>
> down payment
> mortgage
> closing costs

> **tip**
>
> Keep track of your mortgage payments. When your principal drops to the 80% mark, make sure that your PMI is canceled.

activity | **Calculating Down Payments and PMI**

Complete the tasks below.

1. Stacey wants to purchase a house that costs $240,000. If she needs to make a down payment of 20%, how much must she pay?

   _____

2. Jackson made a down payment of 25% on a home costing $185,000. How much did he pay for the down payment?

   _____

3. You are purchasing a house for $100,000. You make a down payment of $10,000. The annual PMI is determined as 0.5% of the loan value. What monthly payment is required to cover the cost of PMI?

   _____

4. Juan is purchasing a house for $200,000. He is making a down payment of 15%, and he is paying PMI at a rate of 0.6% of the loan. What monthly payment is required to cover the cost of PMI?

   _____

Name _____ Date _____

In addition to a down payment, a potential homeowner must also take closing costs into account. **Closing costs** are the fees charged by companies and government offices that process the loan and the sale of the property. They are generally 1% to 8% of the sale price of the home. Some banks will allow buyers to add the closing costs into the mortgage rather than paying them up front.

fyi

You cannot borrow the down payment you make on a house. This money must come from funds you have accumulated.

Closing costs may include, but are not limited to, the following:

- **Sales/brokers commission**   This is a fee paid to the real estate agent who sold you the house.
- **Loan origination fee**   This is a fee to cover the lender's costs for obtaining financing and administrative costs. It is most often expressed as a percentage of the loan amount.
- **Discount Points**   This is a one-time charge that enables the borrower to lower the interest rate on the loan. Generally, the more points, the lower your rate. Each point is 1% of the loan amount. For example, if you have a loan amount of $100,000, one point would cost you $1,000.
- **Appraisal Fee**   This fee covers the cost of evaluating your home to estimate the fair market value.
- **Credit Report Fee**   This fee covers the cost of obtaining a credit report.
- **Lender Inspection Fee**   This fee pays for inspections by the lender or outside inspector of your house/property.
- **Underwriting Fee**   This fee pays for the final analysis and approval of the mortgage.

activity   **Calculating Discount Points**
Answer the questions below.

1. A buyer wants to lower the mortgage rate by purchasing discount points. If the sale price of the home is $200,000, what fee will be charged for 3 discount points? _____

2. What would be the fee for a buyer to purchase 2 discount points on a home with a sale price of $175,000? _____

3. A buyer paid $9,000 to purchase 3 discount points. What was the sale price of the home?

_____

4. The total closing costs for a purchase came to 6.5% of the sale price of the home. If the home cost $225,000, what were the closing costs? _____

5. What would be an advantage of paying closing costs up front rather than adding them into your mortgage? _____

Mortgages

A mortgage is a loan obtained to purchase a home. There are several different types of mortgages. The two most common types are fixed-rate and adjustable-rate.

Fixed-Rate Mortgage

In a **fixed-rate mortgage**, you will owe a certain percentage of the loan as interest to the lender. This amount never changes, and your monthly payment will remain the same over the life of your loan.

The greatest advantage of a fixed-rate mortgage is that it is predictable. You can budget for the future knowing your mortgage payment over the life of the loan. A disadvantage is that the interest rate is generally higher for this predictability. Although you can refinance, or start a new mortgage, if rates drop significantly, you will have to pay closing costs to do so.

Fixed-rate mortgages are generally available in two terms—15 years or 30 years.

- A 30-year term generally has lower payments, but a higher interest rate. With this type of loan, you often have the flexibility to make additional payments and pay the loan early. These are known as prepayments.
- A 15-year term usually has higher payments, but a lower interest rate. It has the advantage that the loan is paid off in half the time of a 30-year term loan.

When you make a mortgage payment each month, part of the payment goes toward the principal and part goes toward interest. Interest can more than double the amount you pay for a home. In fact, for the first several years of the loan, most of the payment goes toward interest. Your ownership, or equity, in the home builds up only as the principal is paid off.

> **key words**
>
> fixed-rate mortgage
> adjustable-rate
>   mortgage (ARM)

> **tip**
>
> Make sure there are no prepayment penalties for any mortgage you are considering.

Name _____ Date _____

Comparing Mortgage Interest Rates

Use the graph below to answer the questions that follow.

The graph below shows the total interest paid for a home with a purchase price of $125,000 at various interest rates.

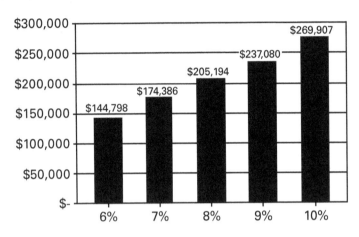

1. What is the total amount paid for the home at the interest rate of 6%?

_____

2. What is the difference in the amount of interest paid as the rate increases from 6% to 10%?

_____

3. At a rate of 8%, about how many times as great as the price of the house is the total amount of interest paid?

_____

4. A buyer has the option to buy a point, thereby lowering the interest rate from 9% to 8% for 1% of the sale price. How much will the buyer pay for the point? By how much will buying the point lower the total amount paid in interest?

_____

Adjustable-Rate Mortgage (ARM)

In an **adjustable-rate mortgage (ARM)**, the interest rate changes to reflect changes in the credit market. The initial rate of the mortgage is fixed for a set amount of time, ranging from 1 month to more than 5 years, and is generally a couple of percentage points below the market rate. This rate is sometimes called "the teaser rate." After the fixed period has passed, the rate automatically increases.

An ARM has a cap, which is the highest interest rate to which the loan can go. For example, if the initial rate is 5% and you have a 4-point cap, the highest your interest rate can go is 9%. In addition, the increase in the interest rate is limited over certain periods of time. This prevents the rate from jumping all four points too quickly. The annual increase is usually limited to one or two percentage points.

The main advantage of an ARM is that the interest rate and the mortgage payments are lower than fixed-rate mortgages in the early years. If you plan to stay in a home for less than 10 years, an ARM might be the best plan for you. The disadvantage is that if you find yourself in a home long term, you assume the risk of changing rates.

> **fyi**
>
> If you are considering an ARM, plan for the worst case. In other words, consider the highest the rate can go and decide if you can afford the payments at that rate.

Convertible Mortgage

This is an ARM loan that allows you to convert to a fixed-rate loan at or before some specified time. This loan lets you start off with a low variable rate but then lets you lock in if fixed rates drop low enough.

Interest-Only Loans

In this type of mortgage, the borrower pays only interest (plus property taxes and homeowner's insurance) on the loan. This results in a lower monthly mortgage payment. Because you are not paying any principal on the loan, the only way to gain equity in your home is if the local housing market increases it. If the market value of your home drops, you could end up owing more than the value of the home.

 Planning with an ARM

Complete the task below.

A homeowner obtains an ARM with an initial rate of 4%. The rate has a 5-point cap, with no increases greater than 2% in any given year.

1. What is the highest rate the homeowner can pay for the loan? _____

2. What is the minimum number of years it will take to reach the cap? _____

Homeowner's Insurance

Once you own a home, you need to obtain homeowner's insurance. This type of insurance is very different from mortgage insurance. Recall that mortgage insurance protects the lender in case a borrower defaults on a loan.

Homeowner's insurance protects your home, possessions, and family in the event of unexpected misfortunes. These might include natural disasters, accidents, or theft. This insurance is designed to enable you to rebuild or replace your property if it becomes damaged.

Most homeowner's policies provide coverage for the following:

- **Dwelling**   Your home plus any attached structures, fixtures, appliances, plumbing, heating, permanent air conditioners, and wiring
- **Other Structures**   Structures that are not directly attached to your home, such as detached garages, storage sheds, fences, driveways, patios, sidewalks, and retaining walls
- **Personal Property**   The contents of your home and other personal items owned by you or family members who live with you
- **Loss of Use**   Your expenses if you can't live in your home while repairs are being made

In addition to property, a homeowner's insurance policy protects you against liability. This is your legal responsibility for any injuries you and your family cause to other people. This includes any damage caused by household pets. Liability insurance provides coverage for the following:

- Your personal liability
- Damage to the property of others
- Medical expenses for injury to others

---

key words

homeowner's insurance

---

fyi

Although most natural disasters are covered by a homeowner's policy, there are some exceptions. Floods and earthquakes, for example, require separate policies.

Name _____ Date _____

Like other insurance policies, a homeowner's policy has a premium that is paid at regular intervals. It also has a deductible. Recall that a deductible is the amount paid before insurance benefits. The premium can be reduced by paying a higher deductible.

 Comparing Deductibles

Choose the best answer to the question.

1. An insurance policy offers a choice. You can pay a premium of $1,260 annually with a deductible of $250 or $1,020 annually with a deductible of $1,000. About how much do you save by agreeing to the higher deductible?

    a. 5%   **b.** 10%   **c.** 20%

When deciding how much homeowner's coverage to choose, you must consider three factors.

Market Value

This is the amount of money a buyer on the open market would pay to purchase your home today.

Replacement Cost

This is what it would cost to rebuild your home if it were totally destroyed. When applied to personal property, replacement cost is the amount of money you would need to replace an item if you were to buy it today. When purchasing structural coverage, it is best to purchase protection to cover the replacement cost of your home. Ideally, you should purchase coverage for 100% of the replacement value of your home. If that is too expensive, you should not get less than 80% of the replacement value of your home.

Actual Cash Value

This is the replacement cost of an item minus an allowance for depreciation. Depreciation is the amount the value of the item has decreased since it was purchased. A basic homeowner's policy covers personal property at actual cash value. You can purchase additional coverage to insure your property for replacement cost.

 Conducting an Inventory

Complete the task below.

2. Taking inventory is how you can decide how much insurance you need. Conduct an inventory of your home, apartment, or room. Record each item you own, its value, and serial number. You should also photograph the rooms, including closets, open drawers, storage buildings, and garage if you have one.

Property Tax

You have found a house. You came up with the down payment, and you can afford the monthly payments. You also budgeted for homeowner's insurance. Is that everything? Not quite. You must account for property taxes. A **property tax** is a fee that the owner of a property pays on the value of the property.

You may see the term *ad-valorem* associated with property tax. **Ad-valorem** describes a tax that is based on the value of something, such as real estate or personal property. Such taxes are used to pay for such municipal expenses as school systems, sewers, parks, libraries, and fire stations.

Property must be appraised periodically to determine if its value has increased or decreased. For example, suppose an owner has a vacant lot. The appraised value will increase after the owner clears the lot and constructs a building on it. Once the value increases, the tax burden associated with the property also increases.

Property tax payments are generally due annually. The annual amount is frequently divided into periodic installments. For homes, it is often charged in monthly installments that are added to mortgage payments.

The property tax rate is usually given as a percentage, which is per one hundred currency units, or per mill, which means out of one-thousandth of a dollar. A mill is one-thousandth of a dollar. To calculate the property tax, the taxing authority multiplies the assessed value of the property by the mill rate and then divides by 1,000.

> **key words**
>
> property tax
> ad-valorem

activity **Calculating Property Tax**

Complete the task below.

1. A property has an assessed value of $50,000. The area where the property is located has a mill rate of 20 mills. What is the annual property tax bill for this property?

_____

2. A property has an assessed value of $100,000 in an area with a mill rate of 25 mills. What is the annual property tax bill for this property?

_____

Name _____   Date _____

Utility Costs

Additional costs that a homeowner must factor into a budget are utilities. **Utilities** are services that you utilize, such as gas, electricity, water, and sewers. They are required in your dwelling, and you must pay for them separately.

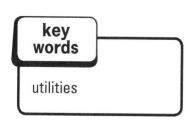

Water

Water rates pay for the cost of operating the water system to provide homeowners with a safe source of drinking water. Customers pay regularly through monthly water bills as well as additional fees such as when their system is first connected. Rates can fluctuate as improvements are made to water facilities as well as during times of peak demand.

The chart below shows the water rate for a particular city in one year. It lists the total charges per HCF, which is one hundred cubic feet of water. That's equal to 748 gallons.

High Season		Low Season						High Season
Q1	Q2				Q3	Q4		
Jul.–Sep.	Oct.	Nov.	Dec.		Jan.–Mar.	Apr.	May	June
$2.141	$2.166	$2.166	$2.166		$2.188	$2.181	$2.181	$2.181

activity   **Calculating Water Costs**

Use the chart above to answer the questions.

1. What is the rate per HCF between January and March?

_____

2. What is the cost of 20 HCF in the month of June?

_____

3. How much more would it cost to use 10 HCF in April than in October?

_____

4. During which quarter is the rate per HCF the least? The greatest?

_____

5. What months are included in the low season?

_____

Name _____   Date _____

Electricity

Whenever you flip on a light switch, push the garage door opener, or turn on your computer, you are using electricity. Electricity is generally measured in kilowatt-hours. A kilowatt (kW) is 1,000 watts. A kilowatt-hour (kWh) describes the use of 1,000 kW for one hour.

Electric companies charge customers by the kilowatt-hour. Rates fluctuate over time and vary by region. To find the cost of using electricity, divide the wattage by 1,000 to find kilowatts. So, for example, an air conditioner that uses about 1,100 watts uses 1.1 kilowatts. Next multiply the number of kilowatts by the number of hours the appliance is used. If the air conditioner is used 5 hours per day, multiply 1.1 kW × 5 h = 5.5 kWh.

To find the number of kilowatt-hours used in one month, multiply by an average of 30 days. So 5.5 kWh × 30 days = 165 kWh/month. Finally multiply this number by the cost per kilowatt-hour. Suppose an electric company charges 7.36 cents per kilowatt-hour, which is $0.0736. You'll find that 165 kWh/month × $0.0736 = $12.14. This means that it costs $12.14 per month to run the air conditioner for 5 hours each day.

activity   Calculating the Cost of Electricity

Find the cost of operating each of the following appliances for one month. Use a cost of 7.36 cents per kilowatt-hour and an average month of 30 days. Round each answer to the nearest cent.

Household Items

Appliance	Approx. wattage	Estimated use	Avg. operating cost/month
Alarm system	6	continuous	1.
Ceiling fan	60	6 hr/day	2.
Computer (including monitor)	40	continuous	3.
Laser printer	1,000	8 hr/month	4.
Lighting—100-watt incandescent bulb	100	6 hr/day	5.
Lighting—40-watt fluorescent tube, 4 ft	40	6 hr/day	6.
TV—big screen	300	6 hr/day	7.

Natural Gas

Some homes use natural gas. If your home does, you should have a meter to measure the amount of gas you have. Each month the meter is read. The previous meter reading is subtracted from the new reading to determine the amount of gas you have used.

To read your meter, begin with the dial on the left. If the hand is between two numbers, always select the lower number. The meter below is read as 6,084.

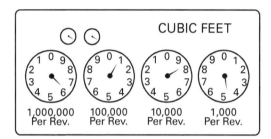

Although bills differ from one company to the next, your gas bill should show the date your meter was read. It should also give the current reading and the previous reading. The meter is generally read in cubic feet of CCF, which is 100 cubic feet of gas.

Many companies convert the readings into units called therms. One cubic foot equals 1,050 BTUs, and one therm is approximately 100,000 BTUs.

 activity   **Reading a Gas Bill**

Review the gas bill on page 46. Use it to answer these questions.

1. What is the account number? _____

2. What is the ID of the meter? _____

3. On what date was the most current reading of the meter? _____

4. How many therms of gas were used since the last reading? _____

5. What is the rate for each therm of gas? _____

6. When is the payment due? _____

7. What is the total amount due? _____

THE GAS COMPANY
ENERGY SERVICES

INVOICE

No. 001234507 1505
Bill Date 7/15/08

Account Name Utility Return of Estimate Gas Customer
Service Address HILO 433 Hoopaia St. 96628
Acct No. 123-45-0 Class U-Res

Service Type U-SNG Metered
or
U-LPG Metered

Contract/P.O.#

SH

Page 1

METER READINGS

Meter ID	···· Last Reading ···· Date	Read	···· Current Reading ···· Date	Read	Read Days	Factor	Therms
79564	5/7/08	3059	7/12/08	3194	66	0 25637	34.61
79564	5/7/08	3059	Return Est.				-18.20
	Net Days This Billing				32	**Therms**	16.41

CURRENT CHARGES

Description	···· Gas Service ···· Therms	Rate	Amount	Other Service Amount	Date
Gas Charges	34.61	$2.9500	$102.10		
Fuel Cost Adjustment	34.61		3.77		
Monthly or Other Periodic Customer Charge			$13.50		
Return of Estimate	-16.20			($62.42)	
Total Current Charges			**$56.35**		

ACCOUNT SUMMARY

Previous Balance	Payments/Adj's	Current Charges	Total Amount Due
$62.42	-$62.42	$56.35	$56.35

Payment Due Date for Current Charges   7/30/08

PLEASE READ!

Put an end to the hassle of writing a check to pay your bill every month. Simplify your life. Sign up for our FREE Automatic Bill Payment service. Call the office nearest you.

or

THIS BILL WILL BE PAID BY AUTOMATIC BILL PAYMENT ON THE DUE DATE.

Detach this portion and mail with payment. Do not detach if paying at the bank or in person.

Acct No. 123-45-0	Bill Date 7/15/08	Payment Due	Amount	Due Date	TOTAL PAYMENT DUE
See reverse side for terms and conditions.		Due from Prior Bill	$0.00	Past Due	
		Current Charges	$56.35	7/30/08	$56.35

2160000013009290000

Make checks payable to:

Utility Return of Estimate Gas Customer
12345 Ipono St.
Kailua, HI 96734

The Gas Company
P. O. Box 3000
Honolulu HI 96392-3000

Amount Paid $ _____

Chapter 3 Review

Use the clues to complete the puzzle.

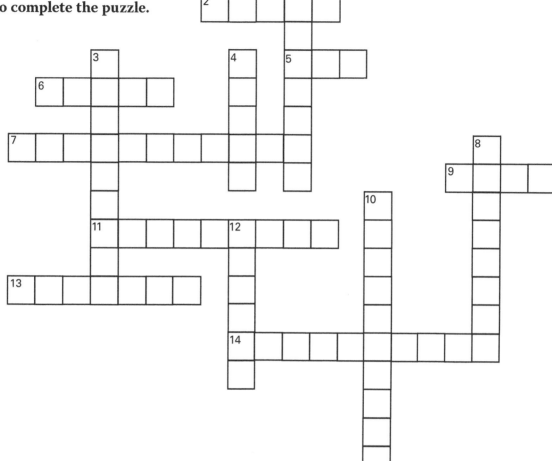

Across

2. The unit in which most gas companies measure the amount of gas you use is the ___.

5. Borrowers who make a down payment of less than 20% must purchase _____ to protect the lender.

6. One kilowatt is one thousand _____.

7. The _____ cost is how much it would be to rebuild your home if it were totally destroyed.

9. The _____ payment is the amount you pay up front when you purchase a home.

11. Homeowner's _____ protects your home, possessions, and family.

13. A buyer must pay _____ costs, such as sales commission, loan origination fees, and discount points.

14. An _____-rate mortgage changes to reflect increases in the credit market.

Down

1. A _____ tax is the fee you pay to fund municipal services based on the value of your home.

3. Gas, electricity, water, and sewers are examples of _____.

4. A _____-rate mortgage stays the same for the life of the loan.

8. The _____ is the amount borrowed to pay for the difference between the price of a home and the down payment.

10. Your _____ is the amount you must pay before the insurance company starts to pay for claims.

12. The _____ cash value is the cost of an item minus any depreciation.

Comprehension

15. How is a fixed lease different from a gross lease?

_____

16. Why does a landlord require a security deposit?

_____

17. List three rights that every renter has.

_____

18. List three responsibilities of every renter.

_____

19. A landlord must have homeowner's insurance. Why should a renter purchase renter's insurance?

_____

20. How is a down payment related to a mortgage?

_____

21. Why do lenders require PMI if a borrower makes a down payment of less than 20%?

_____

22. Why might a potential homeowner purchase discount points?

_____

23. What are the pros and cons of 15- and 30-year fixed-rate mortgages?

_____

24. Why does the amount of the deductible affect the premium of a homeowner's insurance policy?

_____

Extension Activity

Use the local newspaper or visit local banks to compare mortgage rates and terms. Create a chart to summarize your findings. Use another sheet of paper, if necessary.

Name _____ Date _____

Certificates of Deposit

In order to save for the future, you need to invest. To invest is to place funds into some type of account in hopes that the funds will increase in the future. One way to invest is through the use of a **certificate of deposit**. A certificate of deposit, also known as a CD, is a type of savings certificate. An individual deposits a certain amount of money with a bank for a fixed period, usually from one to five years. The person is guaranteed a locked interest rate that is slightly higher than that of a traditional savings account.

A CD is described by a maturity date. The term of a CD generally ranges from one month to five years, but it can be as short as a few days in some cases. It is usually possible to redeem your CD before it matures. If you do, however, you will have to pay an early withdrawal fee or forfeit a portion of the interest earned.

A CD must also list the amount deposited. CDs less than $100,000 are called *small CDs*, whereas those for greater amounts are called *large CDs* or *jumbo CDs*.

For people who want to invest without risk, a CD is an excellent investment option because amounts less than $100,000 are protected by the Federal Deposit Insurance Corporation (FDIC).

There are a couple of things to be cautious about when setting up a CD. The first is to find out if the CD is "callable" or not. If the CD is callable, the bank can end it, forcing you to establish a new CD. This might happen to long-term CDs when interest rates have dropped. As a result, you would lose the higher rate of interest you were counting on. You should also make sure you know when the interest is applied, whether the interest is fixed or variable, and what penalties are incurred if you need to close the CD early.

APR vs. APY

If you shop around for CD rates, you will see two interest values quoted. One is the annual percentage rate (APR), and the other is the annual percentage yield (APY). APR is the simple interest you would earn in one year. APY is the total amount of interest you earn in one year as a result of compound interest.

> key words
>
> certificate of deposit

APR and APY can be a little confusing, but it comes down to when the interest is paid. The more frequently the interest is calculated, the greater the yield will be. If an investment pays interest annually, the APR and the APY are the same. If, however, interest is paid more often, the APY will be greater than the APR.

<table>
<tr><td>tip</td></tr>
<tr><td>Advertisements of a CD's APY can sometimes be misleading. Make sure you know when the interest is compounded relative to the length of the CD.</td></tr>
</table>

Suppose you purchase a one-year CD for $1,000 that pays 5% semi-annually. After 6 months, the CD earns an interest payment of $25. That $25 then earns interest for the next 6 months. It earns an additional $0.625, making the total interest for the next 6 months $25.625. While it may not sound like much, it will add up over time.

When you compare CDs at different banks, you might find a table similar to the one shown below. The term is the length of the CD, or the amount of time until it matures. The rate is the annual percentage rate (APR). The APY is the annual percentage yield. The MIN is the minimum amount you must deposit to take advantage of the rates. Generally, the longer the term or the higher the minimum, the greater the rates.

TERM	RATE	APY	MIN
30 days	4.98%	5.10%	$1,000
60 days	4.98%	5.11%	$1,000
90 days	5.20%	5.30%	$25,000
90 days	5.10%	5.25%	$1,000
6 months	5.33%	5.40%	$1,000
1 year	5.26%	5.40%	$1,000
1 year	5.23%	5.47%	$5,000
2 years	5.35%	5.47%	$5,000
2 years	5.34%	5.48%	$1,000
4 years	5.08%	5.20%	$1,000
5 years	5.21%	5.35%	$1,000

activity   Comparing CDs

Use the table above to answer the questions.

1. By how much does the APY increase when the term of a $1,000 CD is increased from 30 to 90 days? _____

2. By how much does the APY increase when the term of a $1,000 CD is increased from 4 years to 5 years? _____

3. How much greater is the APY than the APR for a $1,000 CD invested for 1 year? _____

4. How much greater is the APY for a $25,000 CD for 90 days than a $1,000 CD for the same term? _____

Stocks

If a company wants to grow, it needs money. One option is to take a loan from a bank, but this would involve paying interest and therefore owing more money. Another option is to issue **stock**. People who buy the stock give the company the money it needs. In return, the stock purchasers own a part of the company. Each part is known as a share. People who own stock are called stockholders or shareholders.

Stockholders in a company have voting rights. They vote on such issues as who will be elected to the board of directors. Generally, stockholders have one vote for each share owned. Stockholders with many shares, therefore, will have a greater influence than stockholders with fewer shares. Keep in mind that a large company can have millions, or even billions, of shares.

Stock can be common stock or preferred stock. Common stock is a simple share of ownership. If the company were to go bankrupt, there would be no financial obligation to common shareholders. The common stock would become worthless. Preferred stock is associated with several advantages. For instance, preferred stock usually has a higher dividend and a large vote in running the company.

Some companies offer a dividend with their stock, while others do not. A dividend is a payment from a portion of the company's profits. Instead of the money being reinvested into the company, it is distributed to shareholders. Most companies that pay a dividend also have dividend reinvestment programs. Instead of taking the dividend as a payment, you can take its value in stock. This would increase the number of your shares of stock.

key words

stock
initial public offering (IPO)

fyi

The term *stock market* refers to the buying and selling of stock. It is not a specific place.

 activity   **Collecting Dividends**

Answer the questions.

1. Suppose you own 100 shares of stock. It pays $1 per share in dividend. How much will you receive every quarter?

_____

2. Randall owns 250 shares of stock. The stock pays $2 per share in dividend. Each share of stock sells for $25. How many new shares of stock can Randall purchase through dividend reinvestment?

_____

Name _____ Date _____

Buying and Selling Stock

A company sells shares to investors in an organized fashion called a public offering. The first public offering is called the **initial public offering (IPO)**. If you buy a share of stock, you may receive a piece of paper called a stock certificate. More and more, stocks are represented electronically rather than with paper certificates.

After the company's IPO, investors can sell their shares or buy more. Shares are traded on organized stock markets such as the New York Stock Exchange and Nasdaq. The most common method of buying and selling stock is through a stockbroker. A stockbroker acts as an agent who matches up stock buyers and sellers.

If a company makes money, the value of its stock goes up. Conversely, if a company loses money, the value of its stock goes down. If you are a stockholder, your investment depends on the value of the stock. If you can sell your stock for a higher price than the price at which you bought it, you make money. If, however, the price drops below the amount you bought it for, you lose money. You must also take into account any fees associated with a sale, such as commission paid to a stockbroker.

fyi

Until 2001, stocks were traded in fractions based on $\frac{1}{8}$. This came from the Spanish trading system that was in common use when the U.S. stock market opened more than 200 years ago. Now stocks are traded in dollars and cents.

activity | **Stock Profits and Losses**

Complete each problem.

1. You bought 100 shares of stock for $20 per share. You sold them for $36 per share. You paid a commission of $75 to the stockbroker for the sale. What was your total profit from the sale?

2. Janice bought 100 shares of stock for $100 per share. She later sold them for $50 per share. If she paid a commission of $100 to the stockbroker for the sale, what was her total loss from the sale?

3. Philip bought 35 shares of stock for $15 per share. He later sold them for $22 per share with a commission of $50 for the sale. What was his total profit on the sale?

4. Regina bought 50 shares of stock at $80 per share. She later sold them for $65 per share. She also had to pay a fee of $50 to her stockbroker. What was her overall loss on the sale?

Bonds

Another type of investment option is a bond. The best way to describe a bond is as an "I.O.U." When you purchase a **bond**, you are essentially lending money to the organization selling the bond. It might be a corporation or a government. In return for the loan, the organization agrees to pay you a specified rate of interest during the life of the bond.

The interest rate is often described as the coupon. When the bond matures, the issuer has to repay the face value of the bond. Bonds are known as fixed-income securities because they specify the exact amount of cash you'll get back if you hold the security until maturity.

Bonds pay interest at set intervals of time. In this way, they can provide income for some people. Consider, for example, a retired individual who owns $100,000 worth of bonds that pay 8% interest annually. That individual would receive $8,000 annually. It would be divided into monthly or quarterly payments that provide a predictable cash flow.

There are many different types of bonds. Here is a review of a few that you might encounter.

```
+----------------+
|   key          |
|   words        |
+----------------+
|   bond         |
+----------------+
```

Municipal Bonds

These bonds are issued by states, cities, counties, and other governmental entities to raise money for such projects as building schools, highways, hospitals, and sewer systems.

Zero Coupon Bonds

These bonds have no coupon, or periodic interest payments. Instead, the investor receives one payment at maturity that is equal to the principal invested plus the interest earned, compounded semiannually.

U.S. Treasury Securities

These include bills, notes, and bonds that involve lending money to the U.S. government for a specified period of time. Because these are backed by the government, they are considered the safest of all investments. As a result, their interest rates are generally lower than other types of bonds.

Corporate Bonds

These bonds are issued by private and public corporations. They are usually issued in multiples of $1,000 and $5,000. The corporation promises to return your principal on a specified maturity date. Until that time, it pays a stated rate of interest, usually semiannually.

Name _____ Date _____

Unlike stock prices, the bond prices you can find online or in the newspaper are not actual dollar prices. They are percentages of something known as the bond's par value, which is usually $1,000 for corporate bonds. The par value of a corporate bond quoted at 99.6% is actually 99.6% of $1,000, or $996. If you buy or sell bonds, you will need to read a bond table similar to the one shown below.

	Coupon	Mat. date	Bid$	Yld%
Corporate				
AGT Lt	8.800	Sep 22/25	100.46	8.75
Air Ca	6.750	Feb 02/04	94.00	9.09
AssCap	5.400	Sep 04/01	100.01	5.38
Avco	5.750	Jun 02/03	100.25	5.63
Bell	6.250	Dec 01/03	101.59	5.63
Bell	6.500	May 09/05	102.01	5.95
BMO	7.000	Jan 28/10	106.55	6.04
BNS	5.400	Apr 01/03	100.31	5.24
BNS	6.250	Jul 16/07	101.56	5.95
CardTr	5.510	Jun 21/03	100.52	5.27
Cdn Pa	5.850	Mar 30/09	93.93	6.83
Clearn	0.000	May 15/08	88.50	8.61
CnCrTr	5.625	Mar 24/05	99.78	5.68
Coke	5.650	Mar 17/04	99.59	5.80

Column 1   Column 2   Column 3   Column 4   Column 5

- Column 1 shows who issued the bond. It might be a company, state, or country.
- Column 2 shows the interest rate on the bond.
- Column 3 lists the maturity date of the bond. Typically, only the last two digits of the year are shown. So 25 means 2025.
- Column 4 gives the bid price. This is what someone is willing to pay for the bond as a percentage.
- Column 5 lists the annual yield until the bond matures.

If you hold the bond to maturity, you are guaranteed to get your principal back. However, if you sell the bond before it matures, you will have to sell it at the going rate. It may be above or below par value. The bond yield is found by dividing the amount of interest it will pay over the course of a year by the current price of the bond.

activity   Calculating Current Yield

Solve the following problems.

1. What is the current yield of a bond that cost $1,000 and pays $75 a year in interest? _____

2. What is the current yield of a bond that cost $1,000 and pays $100 a year in interest? _____

3. What is the current yield of a bond that cost $1,000 and pays $65 a year in interest? _____

4. What is the current yield of a bond that cost $1,000 and pays $50 a year in interest? _____

Name _____ Date _____

Mutual Funds

A **mutual fund** is basically a group of investors who work through a fund manager to purchase a portfolio of stocks or bonds. The fund manager trades the fund's securities, which are the stocks, bonds, and other items. The fund manager then realizes any gains or losses. The investment proceeds are then passed along to individual investors.

key words

mutual fund

You can buy a share of the mutual fund. When you buy a share, you pay the net asset value, or NAV, as well as any sales charges, known as the load. The NAV is calculated every day based on the total value of the fund divided by the number of shares that have been sold.

Changes in the NAV can change your investment. Suppose, for example, you invest $1,000 in a mutual fund with an NAV of $10.00. You will own 100 shares of the fund. If the NAV then drops to $9.00, you will still own 100 shares. However, your investment is now worth $900. Conversely, if the NAV goes up to $11.00, your investment will become worth $1,100 for the same shares.

activity | **Calculating Changes in the NAV**

Answer the questions below.

1. José purchases 80 shares of a mutual fund with an NAV of $2. How much does this purchase cost?

_____

2. Florence spends $2,000 to purchase shares of a mutual fund with an NAV of $16. How many shares does Florence obtain?

_____

3. You spend $3,000 to purchase 250 shares of a mutual fund with an NAV of $12. By how much does your investment decrease if the NAV drops to $10?

_____

4. Thea spends $560 to purchase 280 shares of a mutual fund with an NAV of $2. How much does Thea earn if the NAV rises to $4?

_____

Name _____ Date _____

You might think that selecting a mutual fund is easy compared to selecting your own stocks. This is not necessarily the case. There are over 10,000 different mutual funds. They can be summarized into three main groups.

Money Market Funds

These funds have relatively low risks when compared to other mutual funds. They are limited by law to certain high-quality, short-term investments. Although it does happen, losses with these funds are not common.

Bond Funds

These funds have higher risks than money market funds, but they generally pay higher yields. Unlike money market funds, bond funds are not restricted to high-quality or short-term investments. Bond funds can vary dramatically in terms of risk because there are so many different types of bonds.

Stock Funds

These funds involve more risk than the other two types of funds. However, they can offer the greatest returns. Stock funds are further classified in terms of their goals. A growth fund, for example, works with stocks that have a potential for a large gain but may not pay a regular dividend. An income fund may work with corporate bonds that pay dividends but have a lower potential for gain.

> **fyi**
>
> Many funds are identified by a specific focus. For example, some funds buy only technology stocks. Others might only invest in environmentally friendly companies.

activity **Comparing Mutual Funds**

Complete the following task.

Use the newspaper or Internet to research several mutual funds. For each fund find out its type, what kinds of investments it makes, and the NAV. Organize your findings in a chart.

Money Market

The stock market can be very volatile. Some investors prefer a less risky environment such as the **money market**. The money market is a vehicle through which large institutions and governments manage their short-term cash needs. Money market securities are similar to bonds in that they are fixed-income. The difference is that they are very short term, the securities are traded in very high denominations, and they are not traded on a central floor or exchange.

Individual investors can gain access to the money market through money market mutual funds, as described in the previous lesson, or through money market bank accounts.

A money market bank account is a type of savings account that is similar to a regular savings account. The difference is that the money market account pays a higher interest rate, requires a higher minimum balance, and limits the number of withdrawals each month. In addition, a money market account is similar to a checking account in that you can often write up to three checks a month from the account.

Like other bank accounts, the money in a money market account is insured by the FDIC.

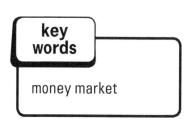

key words

money market

activity   **Opening a Money Market Account**

Use the chart below to answer the questions.

Money Market Account

Balance	Interest Rate	APY
$0–$99	0.00%	0.00%
$100–$9,999	1.64%	1.65%
$10,000–$24,999	3.10%	3.15%
$25,000–$49,999	3.59%	3.66%
$50,000–$99,999	4.16%	4.25%
$100,000+	4.59%	4.70%

1. What APY will you earn for opening an account with $500? _____

2. What APY will you earn for opening an account with $5,000? _____

3. What APY will you earn for opening an account with $15,000? _____

4. What APY will you earn for opening an account with $50,000? _____

Retirement Planning

Someday, after you have worked for many years, you will want to retire. To retire means to withdraw from one's occupation or career. Proper planning can be the difference between enjoying a secure retirement in which you know you can pay your bills and a future in which you will struggle to keep working to support yourself.

It's never too soon to start saving. The sooner you begin saving, the more time your money has to grow.

Be realistic in your goals. Decide how you want to live in retirement and figure out how much it will cost. A rule of thumb suggests that you will need 70% of your pre-retirement income after retirement. However, if you want to travel, build a home, or will require medical care, you may need 100% of your pre-retirement income.

There are three main sources of retirement income. They are social security, pensions, and savings.

> **key words**
>
> pension
> IRA
> 401K

Social Security

Social security is a government program that gives retired and elderly people a monthly amount of money for living, health care, and disability benefits. While you are working, you and your employer pay a portion of each paycheck to the Social Security Administration. This money is set aside until you retire. You can determine your estimated social security benefits upon retirement. If you have not received a statement, you can order one online. The average monthly retirement check is less than $1,000. Social security will help in retirement, but it will most likely not be enough to support most people.

> **fyi**
>
> Political leaders are continually addressing problems with social security. As a result, the future of social security is uncertain. Because of this, you cannot count on social security alone for retirement.

> **activity**
>
> **Estimating Social Security**
>
> **Complete the following task.**

A statement estimates that a person will receive $960 per month through social security. The person earned $4,200 per month before retirement.

1. About what percent of the pre-retirement amount will be replaced by social security?

_____

2. How much more will the person need each month to earn 70% of the pre-retirement amount?

_____

Pension

A **pension** is a plan set up by an employer to help employees save for retirement. An employee usually has to work 5 to 10 years to be part of a pension plan. If you leave the company before that, you may lose any benefits you have accumulated. If you do have benefits, you can often keep the money in that account until you retire. Some companies will let you take the money, but you will have to pay a substantial penalty tax.

IRA

An **IRA**, or Individual Retirement Account, is another way to save for retirement. You can set up this account at a bank, credit union, or other financial institution. There are two types of IRA accounts.

- **Roth IRA**   With this product, you do not receive a tax deduction when you contribute. However, earnings are free of tax when you or your beneficiary withdraws them if you meet certain requirements.

- **Traditional IRA**   With this product, you don't pay income taxes on the earnings and deductible contributions of your IRA until you begin taking withdrawals, usually after you retire.

fyi

Once you have retired, you can stretch your savings by withdrawing from taxable accounts first. Let the interest on tax-advantaged accounts compound as long as possible.

401K

One of the easiest ways to save for retirement is through a **401K** program. This is a retirement plan set up by an employer through an investment company, insurance company, or bank. You can contribute a certain percentage of every paycheck up to a limit without paying taxes on it. Your employer may match your contributions. So for every dollar you contribute, your employer may add another dollar. Your money is then invested in one or more mutual funds.

activity   **Contributing to a 401K**

Complete the task below.

You work for an employer that matches 50¢ for each dollar contribution to a 401K plan. You earn $1,800 per pay period and contribute 2% of earnings to your 401K.

1. How much do you contribute each pay period? _____

2. How much does your employer contribute each pay period? _____

3. What is the total contribution to your 401K each pay period? _____

Chapter 4 Review

Vocabulary

**Match each of the terms on the left to the definition on the right.
Write the letter of the definition on the line provided.**

_____ **1.** CD

_____ **2.** Roth IRA

_____ **3.** Bond

_____ **4.** Money market

_____ **5.** Mutual fund

_____ **6.** IPO

_____ **7.** Pension

_____ **8.** Stock

_____ **9.** APY

_____ **10.** APR

a. A share in a company

b. The simple interest you would earn in one year

c. A plan set up by an employer to help employees save for retirement

d. An account at a bank, credit union, or other financial institution that gives the investor tax-deferred advantages upon retirement

e. A savings product in which a certain amount of money is deposited with a bank for a fixed period during which it earns interest

f. An investment product in which your money is lent to an institution and will be paid back with interest

g. The total amount of interest you earn in one year as a result of compound interest

h. A group of investors who work through a fund manager to purchase a portfolio of stocks or bonds

i. A method for large institutions and governments to manage their short-term cash needs

j. The first public offering for a new stock

Extension Activity

Make a retirement plan for yourself. Use another sheet of paper, if necessary. Write down some of the expenses you expect to have upon retirement. Even if your retirement is far off in the future, think about where you might like to live and what you hope to be doing when you do retire. Based on current expenses, estimate the monthly cost of your retirement.

Name _____ Date _____

Income Taxes

You encounter many different types of taxes. **Income tax** is a tax levied on any money you earn. It is considered a progressive tax because the amount you must pay rises with your income.

By April 15 every year, individuals must report their total income to the Internal Revenue Service (IRS). This includes income from wages, profits from investments, and any winnings. If the gross income is over a certain amount, the individual must file a return. The chart below shows the gross income required for filing for a given year.

income tax
standard deduction

Chart A—For Most People

IF your filing status is . . .	AND at the end of 2006 you were* . . .	THEN file a return if your gross income** was at least . . .
Single	under 65 65 or older	$8,450 9,700
Married filing jointly***	under 65 (both spouses) 65 or older (one spouse) 65 or older (both spouses)	$16,900 17,900 18,900
Married filing separately (see page 17)	any age	$3,300
Head of household (see page 17)	under 65 65 or older	$10,850 12,100
Qualifying widow(er) with dependent child (see page 17)	under 65 65 or older	$13,600 14,600

  * *If you were born on January 1, 1942, you are considered to be age 65 at the end of 2006.*

 ** ***Gross income** means all income you received in the form of money, goods, property, and services that is not exempt from tax, including any income from sources outside the United States (even if you can exclude part or all of it). **Do not** include social security benefits unless you are married filing a separate return and you lived with your spouse at any time in 2006.*

 *** *If you did not live with your spouse at the end of 2006 (or on the date your spouse died) and your gross income was at least $3,300, you must file a return regardless of your age.*

The filing status indicates if you file your taxes with a spouse, alone, or some other way. Tax forms from the IRS include directions describing each filing status.

activity | Determining Filing Requirements

Use the chart above. Write *YES* if the following individuals must file a return and *NO* if they do not need to file a return.

1. A single, 40-year-old woman who earns $12,000 _____

2. A single, 70-year-old man who earns $6,213 _____

3. A married couple who are both under 65 and earn $24,000 combined _____

4. A head of household who earns $9,210 _____

5. A married couple who are both over 65 and earn $45,731 combined _____

www.harcourtschoolsupply.com
© Harcourt Achieve Inc. All rights reserved.

61

Chapter 5: Taxes
Financial Math 2, SV 9781419034381

Standard Deduction

An amount known as the standard deduction is subtracted from the total income when calculating the amount of tax owed. The **standard deduction** is a fixed dollar amount that depends on your filing status. The chart below summarizes the standard deduction for a given year for each filing status for individuals.

If your filing status is:	Your standard tax deduction is:	If 65 or over AND/OR blind add for EACH
Single	$5,150	$1,250
Married filing a joint tax return or Qualifying widow(er) with dependent child	$10,300	$1,000
Married filing a separate tax return	$5,150	$1,000
Head of Household	$7,550	$1,250
Dependent Children	The greater of $850 OR the amount of earned income, plus $300. Not to exceed $5,150 unless the dependent is blind. If blind add $1,250.	

activity **Finding the Standard Deduction**

Use the chart above to answer the questions.

1. Veronica is a 30-year-old single woman. What is her standard deduction? _____

2. Craig is under 65 years of age and is the head of a household. What is his standard deduction?

_____

3. Lucy is married, but she is filing separately from her husband. She is under 65 years old. What is

her standard deduction? _____

4. Alexander and Abigail are a married couple under age 65 filing together. What is their standard

deduction? _____

Calculating Tax

Any amount that remains after the standard deduction is subtracted from the total income is considered taxable income. Once you know your taxable amount, you must consult a chart provided by the IRS that indicates the amount of tax you owe. Some taxpayers must complete a form 1040. The chart is located within the directions provided with this form. A portion of a sample chart is shown on the next page.

Name _____ Date _____

To read the chart, first determine your taxable income, and then find that amount in the chart. For example, suppose you are single and your taxable income is $68,512. Find the row that shows at least 68,500, but less than 68,550. Read over to the column labeled *Single*. Your tax is $13,689.

2006 Tax Table–*Continued*

If line 43 (taxable income) is—		And you are—			
At least	But less than	Single	Married filing jointly *	Married filing sepa-rately	Head of a house-hold
		Your tax is—			
68,000					
68,000	68,050	13,564	10,121	13,749	12,364
68,050	68,100	13,576	10,134	13,763	12,376
68,100	68,150	13,589	10,146	13,777	12,389
68,150	68,200	13,601	10,159	13,791	12,401
68,200	68,250	13,614	10,171	13,805	12,414
68,250	68,300	13,626	10,184	13,819	12,426
68,300	68,350	13,639	10,196	13,833	12,439
68,350	68,400	13,651	10,209	13,847	12,451
68,400	68,450	13,664	10,221	13,861	12,464
68,450	68,500	13,676	10,234	13,875	12,476
68,500	68,550	13,689	10,246	13,889	12,489
68,550	68,600	13,701	10,259	13,903	12,501
68,600	68,650	13,714	10,271	13,917	12,514
68,650	68,700	13,726	10,284	13,931	12,526
68,700	68,750	13,739	10,296	13,945	12,539
68,750	68,800	13,751	10,309	13,959	12,551
68,800	68,850	13,764	10,321	13,973	12,564
68,850	68,900	13,776	10,334	13,987	12,576
68,900	68,950	13,789	10,346	14,001	12,589
68,950	69,000	13,801	10,359	14,015	12,601

If line 43 (taxable income) is—		And you are—			
At least	But less than	Single	Married filing jointly *	Married filing sepa-rately	Head of a house-hold
		Your tax is—			
71,000					
71,000	71,050	14,314	10,871	14,589	13,114
71,050	71,100	14,326	10,884	14,603	13,126
71,100	71,150	14,339	10,896	14,617	13,139
71,150	71,200	14,351	10,909	14,631	13,151
71,200	71,250	14,364	10,921	14,645	13,164
71,250	71,300	14,376	10,934	14,659	13,176
71,300	71,350	14,389	10,946	14,673	13,189
71,350	71,400	14,401	10,959	14,687	13,201
71,400	71,450	14,414	10,971	14,701	13,214
71,450	71,500	14,426	10,984	14,715	13,226
71,500	71,550	14,439	10,996	14,729	13,239
71,550	71,600	14,451	11,009	14,743	13,251
71,600	71,650	14,464	11,021	14,757	13,264
71,650	71,700	14,476	11,034	14,771	13,276
71,700	71,750	14,489	11,046	14,785	13,289
71,750	71,800	14,501	11,059	14,799	13,301
71,800	71,850	14,514	11,071	14,813	13,314
71,850	71,900	14,526	11,084	14,827	13,326
71,900	71,950	14,539	11,096	14,841	13,339
71,950	72,000	14,551	11,109	14,855	13,351

If line 43 (taxable income) is—		And you are—			
At least	But less than	Single	Married filing jointly *	Married filing sepa-rately	Head of a house-hold
		Your tax is—			
74,000					
74,000	74,050	15,064	11,621	15,429	13,864
74,050	74,100	15,076	11,634	15,443	13,876
74,100	74,150	15,089	11,646	15,457	13,889
74,150	74,200	15,101	11,659	15,471	13,901
74,200	74,250	15,115	11,671	15,485	13,914
74,250	74,300	15,129	11,684	15,499	13,926
74,300	74,350	15,143	11,696	15,513	13,939
74,350	74,400	15,157	11,709	15,527	13,951
74,400	74,450	15,171	11,721	15,541	13,964
74,450	74,500	15,185	11,734	15,555	13,976
74,500	74,550	15,199	11,746	15,569	13,989
74,550	74,600	15,213	11,759	15,583	14,001
74,600	74,650	15,227	11,771	15,597	14,014
74,650	74,700	15,241	11,784	15,611	14,026
74,700	74,750	15,255	11,796	15,625	14,039
74,750	74,800	15,269	11,809	15,639	14,051
74,800	74,850	15,283	11,821	15,653	14,064
74,850	74,900	15,297	11,834	15,667	14,076
74,900	74,950	15,311	11,846	15,681	14,089
74,950	75,000	15,325	11,859	15,695	14,101

activity   ## Calculating Income Tax

Use the tax chart above to answer the questions.

1. Andrew and Samantha are filing jointly. Their taxable income is $74,886. How much tax do they owe?

_____

2. Felix is married but filing separately. His taxable income is $68,162. How much tax does he owe?

_____

3. Tamara is single and has a taxable income of $71,445. How much tax does she owe?

_____

4. Roderick is head of a household and earns $68,559. How much tax does he owe?

_____

Refunds or Payment

Remember that taxes are withheld from payrolls by employers. The amount withheld is determined by information completed on your W-4 form. If the amount withheld is higher than the tax owed, the government will send you a refund check. If, however, the tax owed is higher than the amount withheld, you must pay an additional amount to the IRS.

Estimated Taxes

To avoid a hefty tax bill, you can estimate your tax in advance and make sure enough is withheld. To estimate your tax, use a chart similar to the one below. Keep in mind that rates change every year, so you need to use the most recent version of the chart provided by the IRS. You also need to find the chart that matches your filing status.

Filing Status, Married filing jointly

If taxable income is over—	But not over—	The tax is:
$0	$15,100	10% of the amount over $0
$15,100	$61,300	$1,510.00 plus 15% of the amount over 15,100
$61,300	$123,700	$8,440.00 plus 25% of the amount over 61,300
$123,700	$188,450	$24,040.00 plus 28% of the amount over 123,700
$188,450	$336,550	$42,170.00 plus 33% of the amount over 188,450
$336,550	no limit	$91,043.00 plus 35% of the amount over 336,550

To find the estimated tax, taxpayers must find the range of their income on the chart. They then use the following formula:

Estimated Tax = Base Tax + (Rate × Amount Over)

For example, suppose Fred and Lisa Jones are married taxpayers with a taxable income of $130,000. Their base tax is $24,040. Their rate is 28%, and they are over by $6,300. Their estimated tax is:

$24,040 + (0.28 × $6,300) = $25,804

 Calculating Estimated Tax

Complete the following problem.

Marianne and Luis are married and filing jointly. Their taxable income is $192,000. Calculate their estimated tax.

W-2 Form

If you work, you must receive a **W-2** form from your employer at the beginning of each year. If you have more than one job, you will receive a W-2 form from each employer. The form must be mailed out by January 31. On this form, your employer reports wages, tax withholdings, and other vital information. The form is sent to you and to the government.

Below is a W-2 form with a brief summary of the major information that belongs on the form.

key words

W-2

tip

When you receive your W-2, verify all of the information— especially your social security number.

Box a	This box contains a nine-digit employee social security number that is unique for each employee at a company.	Box 1	Wages, tips, other compensation. This is the amount that will be entered on the wages line of your tax return.
Box b	Employer's identification number	Box 2	Federal income tax withheld
Box c	Employer's name, address, and ZIP code	Box 3	Social security wages
Box d	Control number	Box 4	Social security tax withheld
Box e	Employee's name	Box 5	Medicare wages and tips
Box f	Employee's address	Box 6	Medicare tax withheld
		Box 9	Advance EIC payment
		Box 10	Dependent care benefits

Name _____ Date _____

activity   **Reading a W-2 Form**

Use the W-2 form to answer the questions.

22222	**a** Employee's social security number 000-00-0000		OMB No. 1545-0008		

b Employer identification number (EIN) 95-6006143-W	**1** Wages, tips, other compensation 12,929.79	**2** Federal income tax withheld 856.11
c Employer's name, address, and ZIP code	**3** Social security wages .00	**4** Social security tax withheld .00
Freezy Ice Cream Co. Payroll Office 10920 Wilshire Blvd. #620 Los Angeles, CA 90024-6508	**5** Medicare wages and tips 13,755.00	**6** Medicare tax withheld 199.45
	7 Social security tips .00	**8** Allocated tips .00
d Control number 123456789	**9** Advance EIC payment .00	**10** Dependent care benefits .00
e Employee's first name and initial Last name Suff.	**11** Nonqualified plans .00	**12a** Code
Logan Whiley 825 Westwood Blvd. Los Angeles, CA 90024	**13** Statutory employee ☐ Retirement plan ☐ Third-party sick pay ☐	**12b** Code
	14 Other DCP-CAS 1,031.64	**12c** Code
		12d Code
f Employee's address and ZIP code		

15 State Employer's state ID number	**16** State wages, tips, etc.	**17** State income tax	**18** Local wages, tips, etc.	**19** Local income tax	**20** Locality name
CA 45-230568	12,929.79	200.98			

Form **W-2** Wage and Tax Statement   **2007**   Department of the Treasury—Internal Revenue Service

Copy 1—For State, City, or Local Tax Department

1. What are the total wages, tips, and compensation for this employee? _____

2. What amount was withheld for federal taxes? _____

3. What amount was withheld for Medicare tax? _____

4. What amount was withheld for social security tax? _____

5. In what state does this employee work? _____

6. For what company does the employee work? _____

Tax Form 1040EZ

Many taxpayers can complete a shortened version of the tax form, known as the **1040EZ**. You can use the 1040EZ if you meet the following requirements:

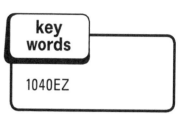

- Your filing status is single or married filing jointly.
- Your taxable income is less than $100,000.
- You do not claim any dependents.
- You had only wages, salaries, tips, taxable scholarship or fellowship grants, unemployment compensation, or Alaska Permanent Fund dividends, and your taxable interest was not over $1,500.

Review the 1040EZ form on page 69 as you review each specific part of the form.

Line 1   Enter the total amount of your wages, salaries, and tips. If you're filing a joint return, also include your spouse's income. For most people, the amount to enter on this line should be shown on their Form(s) W-2 in box 1.

Line 2   Anyone from whom you have earned taxable interest should send you a Form 1099-INT or Form 1099-OID. Include taxable interest from banks, savings and loan associations, money market certificates, credit unions, and savings bonds.

Line 3   If you received unemployment compensation, you should receive Form 1099-G showing the total unemployment compensation paid to you. Enter the amount on the form.

Line 7   Enter the total amount of federal income tax withheld. This should be shown on your 2006 Form(s) W-2 in box 2. If you received a 2006 Form 1099-INT, 1099-G, or 1099-OID showing federal income tax withheld, include the tax withheld in the total on line 7. This tax should be shown in box 4 of these forms.

Lines 8a and 8b   The EIC is a credit for certain people who work and have a qualifying child. The credit may give you a refund even if you do not owe any tax. Follow the directions to see if you qualify for this credit.

Name _____ Date _____

Fill in the form on page 69. Use your name and address along with the following information and chart.

Filing status: single

No dependents

Wages, salary, and tips = $46,000

Taxable interest = $192

No unemployment compensation

No EIC

Federal tax withheld: $5,850

If Form 1040EZ, line 6, is—		And you are—	
At least	But less than	Single	Married filing jointly
		Your tax is—	
37,000			
37,000	37,050	5,814	4,799
37,050	37,100	5,826	4,806
37,100	37,150	5,839	4,814
37,150	37,200	5,851	4,821
37,200	37,250	5,864	4,829
37,250	37,300	5,876	4,836
37,300	37,350	5,889	4,844
37,350	37,400	5,901	4,851
37,400	37,450	5,914	4,859
37,450	37,500	5,926	4,866
37,500	37,550	5,939	4,874
37,550	37,600	5,951	4,881
37,600	37,650	5,964	4,889
37,650	37,700	5,976	4,896
37,700	37,750	5,989	4,904
37,750	37,800	6,001	4,911
37,800	37,850	6,014	4,919
37,850	37,900	6,026	4,926
37,900	37,950	6,039	4,934
37,950	38,000	6,051	4,941

Name _____ Date _____

Form
1040EZ

Department of the Treasury—Internal Revenue Service

Income Tax Return for Single and Joint Filers With No Dependents (99) **2006**

OMB No. 1545-0074

Label
(See page 11.)

Use the IRS label.
Otherwise, please print or type.

L A B E L H E R E	Your first name and initial	Last name	Your social security number
	If a joint return, spouse's first name and initial	Last name	Spouse's social security number
	Home address (number and street). If you have a P.O. box, see page 11.	Apt. no.	▲ You **must** enter your SSN(s) above. ▲
	City, town or post office, state, and ZIP code. If you have a foreign address, see page 11.		Checking a box below will not change your tax or refund.

Presidential Election Campaign (page 11) ▶

Check here if you, or your spouse if a joint return, want $3 to go to this fund . . . . ▶ ☐ **You**   ☐ **Spouse**

Income

Attach Form(s) W-2 here.

Enclose, but do not attach, any payment.

1	Wages, salaries, and tips. This should be shown in box 1 of your Form(s) W-2. Attach your Form(s) W-2.	1	
2	Taxable interest. If the total is over $1,500, you cannot use Form 1040EZ.	2	
3	Unemployment compensation and Alaska Permanent Fund dividends (see page 13).	3	
4	Add lines 1, 2, and 3. This is your **adjusted gross income.**	4	
5	If someone can claim you (or your spouse if a joint return) as a dependent, check the applicable box(es) below and enter the amount from the worksheet on back. ☐ **You** ☐ **Spouse** If no one can claim you (or your spouse if a joint return), enter $8,450 if **single**; $16,900 if **married filing jointly.** See back for explanation.	5	
6	Subtract line 5 from line 4. If line 5 is larger than line 4, enter -0-. This is your **taxable income.** ▶	6	

Payments and tax

7	Federal income tax withheld from box 2 of your Form(s) W-2.	7	
8a	**Earned income credit (EIC).**	8a	
b	Nontaxable combat pay election.	8b	
9	Credit for federal telephone excise tax paid. Attach Form 8913 if required.	9	
10	Add lines 7, 8a, and 9. These are your **total payments.** ▶	10	
11	**Tax.** Use the amount on **line 6 above** to find your tax in the tax table on pages 24–32 of the booklet. Then, enter the tax from the table on this line.	11	

Refund

Have it directly deposited! See page 18 and fill in 12b, 12c, and 12d or Form 8888.

12a	If line 10 is larger than line 11, subtract line 11 from line 10. This is your **refund.** If Form 8888 is attached, check here ▶ ☐	12a	
▶ b	Routing number		▶ c Type: ☐ Checking ☐ Savings
▶ d	Account number		

Amount you owe

| 13 | If line 11 is larger than line 10, subtract line 10 from line 11. This is the **amount you owe.** For details on how to pay, see page 19. ▶ | 13 | |

Third party designee

Do you want to allow another person to discuss this return with the IRS (see page 20)? ☐ **Yes.** Complete the following. ☐ **No**

Designee's name ▶ _____   Phone no. ▶ ( )   Personal identification number (PIN) ☐☐☐☐☐

Sign here

Joint return? See page 11.

Keep a copy for your records.

Under penalties of perjury, I declare that I have examined this return, and to the best of my knowledge and belief, it is true, correct, and accurately lists all amounts and sources of income I received during the tax year. Declaration of preparer (other than the taxpayer) is based on all information of which the preparer has any knowledge.

Your signature	Date	Your occupation	Daytime phone number ( )
Spouse's signature. If a joint return, **both** must sign.	Date	Spouse's occupation	

Paid preparer's use only

Preparer's signature ▶		Date	Check if self-employed ☐	Preparer's SSN or PTIN
Firm's name (or yours if self-employed), address, and ZIP code ▶			EIN	
			Phone no. ( )	

For Disclosure, Privacy Act, and Paperwork Reduction Act Notice, see page 22.

Cat. No. 11329W

Form **1040EZ** (2006)

Tax Form 1040A

The **1040A** is another short form of the Form 1040. It is for taxpayers with taxable income less than $100,000 and income only from the following sources:

- Wages, salaries, tips
- Interest and ordinary dividends
- Capital gain distributions
- Taxable scholarship and fellowship grants
- Pensions, annuities, and IRAs
- Unemployment compensation
- Taxable social security and railroad retirement benefits
- Alaska Permanent Fund dividends
- Jury duty pay

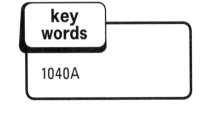

key words

1040A

activity   **Completing Form 1040A**

Fill in the form on pages 71 and 72. Use your name and address along with the information and chart below.

Filing status: single

No dependents

Wages, salary, and tips = $28,000

Taxable interest = $246

Unemployment compensation = $110

No EIC

Federal tax withheld: $3,782

If Form 1040A, line 27, is—		And you are—			
At least	But less than	Single	Married filing jointly *	Married filing sepa- rately	Head of a house- hold
			Your tax is—		
23,000					
23,000	23,050	3,076	2,699	3,076	2,916
23,050	23,100	3,084	2,706	3,084	2,924
23,100	23,150	3,091	2,714	3,091	2,931
23,150	23,200	3,099	2,721	3,099	2,939
23,200	23,250	3,106	2,729	3,106	2,946
23,250	23,300	3,114	2,736	3,114	2,954
23,300	23,350	3,121	2,744	3,121	2,961
23,350	23,400	3,129	2,751	3,129	2,969
23,400	23,450	3,136	2,759	3,136	2,976
23,450	23,500	3,144	2,766	3,144	2,984
23,500	23,550	3,151	2,774	3,151	2,991
23,550	23,600	3,159	2,781	3,159	2,999
23,600	23,650	3,166	2,789	3,166	3,006
23,650	23,700	3,174	2,796	3,174	3,014
23,700	23,750	3,181	2,804	3,181	3,021
23,750	23,800	3,189	2,811	3,189	3,029
23,800	23,850	3,196	2,819	3,196	3,036
23,850	23,900	3,204	2,826	3,204	3,044
23,900	23,950	3,211	2,834	3,211	3,051
23,950	24,000	3,219	2,841	3,219	3,059

Name _____ Date _____

Form

1040A

Department of the Treasury—Internal Revenue Service

U.S. Individual Income Tax Return (99) **2006**

IRS Use Only—Do not write or staple in this space.

Label (See page 18.)	L A B E L	Your first name and initial	Last name		OMB No. 1545-0074
					Your social security number
Use the IRS label. Otherwise, please print or type.	H E R E	If a joint return, spouse's first name and initial	Last name		**Spouse's social security number**
		Home address (number and street). If you have a P.O. box, see page 18.		Apt. no.	▲ You **must** enter your SSN(s) above. ▲
		City, town or post office, state, and ZIP code. If you have a foreign address, see page 18.			Checking a box below will not change your tax or refund.

Presidential Election Campaign ▶ Check here if you, or your spouse if filing jointly, want $3 to go to this fund (see page 18) ▶ ☐ **You** ☐ **Spouse**

Filing status
Check only one box.

1 ☐ Single
2 ☐ Married filing jointly (even if only one had income)
3 ☐ Married filing separately. Enter spouse's SSN above and full name here. ▶
4 ☐ Head of household (with qualifying person). (See page 19.) If the qualifying person is a child but not your dependent, enter this child's name here. ▶
5 ☐ Qualifying widow(er) with dependent child (see page 20)

Exemptions

If more than six dependents, see page 21.

6a ☐ **Yourself.** If someone can claim you as a dependent, **do not** check box 6a.
 b ☐ **Spouse**
 c **Dependents:**

(1) First name Last name	(2) Dependent's social security number	(3) Dependent's relationship to you	(4) ✓ if qualifying child for child tax credit (see page 21)
			☐
			☐
			☐
			☐
			☐
			☐

Boxes checked on 6a and 6b ____

No. of children on 6c who:
• lived with you ____
• did not live with you due to divorce or separation (see page 22) ____

Dependents on 6c not entered above ____

 d Total number of exemptions claimed.

Add numbers on lines above ▶ ☐

Income

Attach Form(s) W-2 here. Also attach Form(s) 1099-R if tax was withheld.

If you did not get a W-2, see page 24.

Enclose, but do not attach, any payment.

7 Wages, salaries, tips, etc. Attach Form(s) W-2. — 7

8a **Taxable** interest. Attach Schedule 1 if required. — 8a
 b **Tax-exempt** interest. **Do not** include on line 8a. — 8b

9a Ordinary dividends. Attach Schedule 1 if required. — 9a
 b Qualified dividends (see page 25). — 9b

10 Capital gain distributions (see page 25). — 10

11a IRA distributions. — 11a   **11b** Taxable amount (see page 25). — 11b

12a Pensions and annuities. — 12a   **12b** Taxable amount (see page 26). — 12b

13 Unemployment compensation, Alaska Permanent Fund dividends, and jury duty pay. — 13

14a Social security benefits. — 14a   **14b** Taxable amount (see page 28). — 14b

15 Add lines 7 through 14b (far right column). This is your **total income.** ▶ 15

Adjusted gross income

16 Penalty on early withdrawal of savings (see page 28). — 16

17 IRA deduction (see page 28). — 17

18 Student loan interest deduction (see page 31). — 18

19 Jury duty pay you gave your employer (see page 31). — 19

20 Add lines 16 through 19. These are your **total adjustments.** — 20

21 Subtract line 20 from line 15. This is your **adjusted gross income.** ▶ 21

For Disclosure, Privacy Act, and Paperwork Reduction Act Notice, see page 58.   Cat. No. 11327A   Form **1040A** (2006)

Form 1040A (2006)   Page **2**

Tax, credits, and payments	**22**	Enter the amount from line 21 (adjusted gross income).		22	

Standard Deduction for—

• People who checked any box on line 23a or 23b **or** who can be claimed as a dependent, see page 32.

• All others:

Single or Married filing separately, $5,150

Married filing jointly or Qualifying widow(er), $10,300

Head of household, $7,550

23a	Check if:	☐ **You** were born before January 2, 1942, ☐ Blind ⎱ **Total boxes** ☐ **Spouse** was born before January 2, 1942, ☐ Blind ⎰ **checked ▶** 23a		☐	
b		If you are married filing separately and your spouse itemizes deductions, see page 32 and check here ▶ 23b		☐	
24		Enter your **standard deduction** (see left margin).		24	
25		Subtract line 24 from line 22. If line 24 is more than line 22, enter -0-.		25	
26		If line 22 is over $112,875, or you provided housing to a person displaced by Hurricane Katrina, see page 32. Otherwise, multiply $3,300 by the total number of exemptions claimed on line 6d.	26		
27		Subtract line 26 from line 25. If line 26 is more than line 25, enter -0-. This is your **taxable income.** ▶		27	
28		**Tax,** including any alternative minimum tax (see page 32).		28	
29		Credit for child and dependent care expenses. Attach Schedule 2.	29		
30		Credit for the elderly or the disabled. Attach Schedule 3.	30		
31		Education credits. Attach Form 8863.	31		
32		Retirement savings contributions credit. Attach Form 8880.	32		
33		Child tax credit (see page 37). Attach Form 8901 if required.	33		
34		Add lines 29 through 33. These are your **total credits.**		34	
35		Subtract line 34 from line 28. If line 34 is more than line 28, enter -0-.		35	
36		Advance earned income credit payments from Form(s) W-2, box 9.		36	
37		Add lines 35 and 36. This is your **total tax.** ▶		37	
38		Federal income tax withheld from Forms W-2 and 1099.	38		
39		2006 estimated tax payments and amount applied from 2005 return.	39		

If you have a qualifying child, attach Schedule EIC.

40a		**Earned income credit (EIC).**	40a		
b		Nontaxable combat pay election. 40b			
41		Additional child tax credit. Attach Form 8812.	41		
42		Credit for federal telephone excise tax paid. Attach Form 8913 if required.	42		
43		Add lines 38, 39, 40a, 41, and 42. These are your **total payments.** ▶		43	

Refund	**44**	If line 43 is more than line 37, subtract line 37 from line 43. This is the amount you **overpaid.**		44	

Direct deposit? See page 53 and fill in 45b, 45c, and 45d or Form 8888.

45a	Amount of line 44 you want **refunded to you.** If Form 8888 is attached, check here ▶ ☐		45a	
▶ b	Routing number ☐☐☐☐☐☐☐☐☐ ▶ **c** Type: ☐ Checking ☐ Savings			
▶ d	Account number ☐☐☐☐☐☐☐☐☐☐☐☐☐☐☐☐☐			
46	Amount of line 44 you want **applied to your 2007 estimated tax.**	46		

Amount you owe	**47**	**Amount you owe.** Subtract line 43 from line 37. For details on how to pay, see page 54. ▶		47	
	48	Estimated tax penalty (see page 54).	48		

Third party designee	Do you want to allow another person to discuss this return with the IRS (see page 55)? ☐ **Yes.** Complete the following. ☐ **No**

Designee's name ▶	Phone no. ▶ ( )	Personal identification number (PIN) ▶ ☐☐☐☐☐

Sign here

Under penalties of perjury, I declare that I have examined this return and accompanying schedules and statements, and to the best of my knowledge and belief, they are true, correct, and accurately list all amounts and sources of income I received during the tax year. Declaration of preparer (other than the taxpayer) is based on all information of which the preparer has any knowledge.

Joint return? See page 18. Keep a copy for your records.

Your signature	Date	Your occupation	Daytime phone number ( )
Spouse's signature. If a joint return, **both** must sign.	Date	Spouse's occupation	

Paid preparer's use only	Preparer's signature ▶		Date	Check if self-employed ☐	Preparer's SSN or PTIN
	Firm's name (or yours if self-employed), address, and ZIP code ▶			EIN	
				Phone no. ( )	

Form **1040A** (2006)

Itemized Deductions

When calculating income tax, certain personal expenses are allowed as deductions from the adjusted gross income. These are known as **itemized deductions**. A taxpayer who itemizes deductions may not claim the standard deduction. The final tax should be calculated both ways to determine which is in the taxpayer's favor.

> **key words**
>
> itemized deductions

Itemized deductions include the following:

Medical Expenses

Medical and dental expenses are generally deductible to the extent they exceed 7.5% of your income. Common expenses include:

- adoption
- doctor/dentist fees
- drug/alcohol treatment
- guide dog costs
- handicap access devices for disabled
- hospital fees
- insurance premiums

- prescriptions
- medical devices
- operations
- organ donation
- physician diet/health programs
- psychiatric care
- school and/or home for disabled

Taxes

The following taxes are generally 100% deductible.

- state/local taxes
- property taxes
- payments to mandatory state funds
- foreign income taxes

- real estate taxes
- value-based auto license fee
- general state/local sales tax

Interest

While most personal interest is no longer deductible, there are still interest expense deductions available to you.

- home mortgage interest
- second home mortgage interest
- home equity loan interest
- interest on special assessments (as real estate tax)

- business interest
- investment interest
- "points" paid

Charitable Contributions

Money or property donated to qualified organizations can be deductible. Qualified organizations include:

- churches
- non-profit schools
- non-profit hospitals
- public parks
- Boy Scouts and Girl Scouts
- war/veterans groups
- agencies such as Red Cross, Salvation Army, Goodwill
- YMCA/YWCA
- some environmental/conservation groups

Schedule A

Itemized deductions are reported on Schedule A, Form 1040. Review the Schedule A on the following page as specific lines are described.

Line 1   Include the total of your medical and dental expenses minus a reimbursement by insurance companies.

Line 5   Include any state and local income taxes withheld.

Line 6   Include taxes paid on real estate not used for business.

Line 7   Include personal property taxes.

Lines 10 and 11   Enter mortgage interest and points.

 Using a Schedule A

Fill out the Schedule A on the following page with the information below.

Total medical expenses = $5,400

State or local income taxes = $0

Real estate taxes = $2,340

Personal property taxes = $1,500

Mortgage interest = $17,000

Charitable gifts by cash = $1,200

Adjusted gross income = $93,000

Name _____ Date _____

SCHEDULES A&B
(Form 1040)

Department of the Treasury
Internal Revenue Service (99)

Schedule A—Itemized Deductions

(Schedule B is on back)

► Attach to Form 1040. ► See Instructions for Schedules A&B (Form 1040).

OMB No. 1545-0074

2006

Attachment
Sequence No. **07**

Name(s) shown on Form 1040 | Your social security number

Medical and Dental Expenses		Caution. Do not include expenses reimbursed or paid by others.			
	1	Medical and dental expenses (see page A-1) . . .	**1**		
	2	Enter amount from Form 1040, line 38 ⌊ **2** ⌋			
	3	Multiply line 2 by 7.5% (.075) . . .	**3**		
	4	Subtract line 3 from line 1. If line 3 is more than line 1, enter -0-		**4**	
Taxes You Paid (See page A-3.)	5	State and local income taxes	**5**		
	6	Real estate taxes (see page A-3)	**6**		
	7	Personal property taxes	**7**		
	8	Other taxes. List type and amount ► _____ _____	**8**		
	9	Add lines 5 through 8		**9**	
Interest You Paid (See page A-3.) Note. Personal interest is not deductible.	10	Home mortgage interest and points reported to you on Form 1098	**10**		
	11	Home mortgage interest not reported to you on Form 1098. If paid to the person from whom you bought the home, see page A-3 and show that person's name, identifying no., and address ► _____ _____	**11**		
	12	Points not reported to you on Form 1098. See page A-4 for special rules	**12**		
	13	Investment interest. Attach Form 4952 if required. (See page A-4.)	**13**		
	14	Add lines 10 through 13		**14**	
Gifts to Charity If you made a gift and got a benefit for it, see page A-4.	15	Gifts by cash or check. If you made any gift of $250 or more, see page A-5 . . .	**15**		
	16	Other than by cash or check. If any gift of $250 or more, see page A-5. You **must** attach Form 8283 if over $500	**16**		
	17	Carryover from prior year	**17**		
	18	Add lines 15 through 17		**18**	
Casualty and Theft Losses	19	Casualty or theft loss(es). Attach Form 4684. (See page A-6.)		**19**	
Job Expenses and Certain Miscellaneous Deductions (See page A-6.)	20	Unreimbursed employee expenses—job travel, union dues, job education, etc. Attach Form 2106 or 2106-EZ if required. (See page A-6.) ► _____	**20**		
	21	Tax preparation fees	**21**		
	22	Other expenses—investment, safe deposit box, etc. List type and amount ► _____ _____	**22**		
	23	Add lines 20 through 22	**23**		
	24	Enter amount from Form 1040, line 38 ⌊ **24** ⌋			
	25	Multiply line 24 by 2% (.02)	**25**		
	26	Subtract line 25 from line 23. If line 25 is more than line 23, enter -0-		**26**	
Other Miscellaneous Deductions	27	Other—from list on page A-7. List type and amount ► _____ _____		**27**	
Total Itemized Deductions	28	Is Form 1040, line 38, over $150,500 (over $75,250 if married filing separately)?			
		☐ **No.** Your deduction is not limited. Add the amounts in the far right column for lines 4 through 27. Also, enter this amount on Form 1040, line 40.			
		☐ **Yes.** Your deduction may be limited. See page A-7 for the amount to enter.	►	**28**	
	29	If you elect to itemize deductions even though they are less than your standard deduction, check here ► ☐			

For Paperwork Reduction Act Notice, see Form 1040 instructions.   Cat. No. 11330X   Schedule A (Form 1040) 2006

Chapter 5 Review
Comprehension

1. By what date are income taxes due each year?

_____

2. What is one reason why some people are exempt from paying taxes?

_____

_____

3. What is a standard deduction?

_____

_____

4. What does an employer report on a W-2 form?

_____

_____

5. Which of the following taxpayers cannot use a 1040EZ?

   a. Man filing as head of household who earns $15,000

   b. Woman who files single and earns $45,000

   c. Married couple with three dependents

   d. Man filing single with itemized deductions

   e. Married couple filing jointly with income of $80,000

   f. Married man with an income of $55,000 filing separately from wife

6. List 3 examples of expenses that can be used as itemized deductions.

_____

_____

_____

Extension Activity

Use your income, if any, from last year to decide if you need to file income taxes. If so, decide which form you need to complete.

Buying a Car

You need to buy a car. How do you decide whether to buy a new car or a used car? The answer that is right for you depends on several considerations.

A new car will generally have fewer problems than a used car. As a car gets older, parts wear out and may require repairs. New cars generally do not have these problems, and if they do, they are often covered under the warranty.

A **warranty** is a promise to repair problems with the car within a certain period of time. Some warranties cover the car for a certain number of miles. Others are for a number of years or a number of miles. For example, a warranty may cover the car for 7 years or 70,000 miles, whichever comes first. A good warranty can protect a car owner from expensive repairs.

A disadvantage of a new car is that it loses about 40% of its value within the first 3 years. In other words, the car depreciates. With a used car, the previous owner absorbed the greatest part of the depreciation.

In addition to depreciation having slowed down, an advantage of a used car is that it costs less than a new car. Used cars are also cheaper to insure and register than new cars.

key words
warranty

activity — Comparing a New Car with a Used Car

James is comparing a new car with a used car. He made this table to summarize what he discovered. Write a paragraph summarizing the comparison.

	New Car	Used Car
Price	$14,500	$7,000
Warranty	5 years	none
Insurance premium	$750	$480
Registration	$70	$40
Age	New	4 years
Mileage	20 miles	36,000 miles

_____

_____

_____

_____

_____

Name _____ Date _____

Paying for a Car

No matter what type of car you decide to buy, you will need to pay for it.
There are three options when paying for a car: cash, loan, or lease.

Cash

The easiest way to pay for a car is by using cash. This prevents you from
paying interest and other fees. A car, however, is an expensive purchase. Many
people do not have enough cash available to purchase a car in this manner.

Loan

Like any other type of loan, a car loan is an agreement to borrow money
and pay it back with interest over a regular schedule. The interest rate
depends on the cost of the car as well as your credit history.

There are two basic types of car loans: long term and short term. Lending
companies generally offer long-term loans only on new cars. A long-term
loan might be for 36, 48, or 60 months. Loans for used vehicles are
generally available only for shorter terms, such as 24 or 36 months.

Longer-term plans generally carry a smaller monthly payment. However,
you will pay more over the life of the loan. As an example, consider that
extending a 3-year $15,000 loan to 4 years will decrease the monthly
payment from $450 to $377. Because the interest rate will increase,
though, the total amount of the loan increases from $16,200 to $18,096.

activity **Car Loan Payments**

**Polly wants to spend about $325 per month on a car loan. The amount she can
afford to finance depends on her credit history. Answer the questions below to
see how the interest rate affects the amount she can finance.**

1. Polly has a low credit score, so she is offered an interest rate of 20.95% on a car loan. She finances
   $12,000 and makes a monthly payment of $324.30 for 60 months. How much does she pay in interest
   on this loan?

   _____

2. Polly has a fair credit score, so she is offered an interest rate of 7.89% on a 60-month car loan. She
   can finance $16,000 to make monthly payments of $323.58. How much does she pay in interest on
   this loan?

   _____

3. Polly has an average credit score, so she is offered an interest rate of 5.55%. She can finance $17,000
   to make a monthly payment of $325.11 for 60 months. How much does she pay in interest on
   this loan?

   _____

Lease

A lease is an agreement to make regular scheduled payments for a specified period of time. At the end of the lease, however, you do not own the car. You have an option to buy it, but the purchase price plus the lease payments made is usually much higher than if you had purchased the car initially.

Deciding to Buy or Lease

When you buy a car using a loan, you pay for the entire cost of the vehicle, plus interest. When you lease, you pay for only a portion of a vehicle's cost. This is the part that you "use up" during the time you're driving it.

Consider buying a car for $20,000. Suppose, instead, you lease the car. The car is estimated to have a value of $13,000 at the end of the lease term. Throughout your lease, then, you pay the $7,000 difference between the original value and the final value of the car. Your payments will be lower than if you buy the car, but you will not own anything at the end of the lease.

activity	**Comparing Loans and Leases**

Use the chart comparing loans and a lease to answer the question.

	Lease	0% Loan	6% Loan
Car Price	$23,000	$23,000	$23,000
Down Payment	$1,000	$1,000	$1,000
Interest Rate	6%	0%	6%
Residual Value	$11,000	n/a	n/a
Months	36	36	36
Payment	**$388.06**	**$611.11**	**$669.28**

Write a short paragraph explaining how the lease compares with the two loans.

_____

_____

_____

_____

_____

_____

Name _____ Date _____

Auto Insurance

Aside from a home, a car is probably one of the most expensive items you will own. Auto insurance protects your investment in your car and gives you a way to deal with the expense of accidents, vandalism, or theft. In most states, auto insurance is required before you can even register a car. Auto insurance is divided into several types of coverage.

- **Collision insurance**   This covers damage to your own vehicle incurred in an accident. Collision insurance will cover the driver whether or not he or she is at fault for the accident. It also provides for towing, storage, and salvage if the car has been badly damaged. Generally, collision insurance will cover the cost of repairs to the vehicle, or replacement if it is badly damaged.

- **General liability insurance**   This covers damages you might cause to other people's property as well as injuries to the people themselves.

- **Comprehensive insurance**   This covers fire damage to your vehicle, break-ins, vandalism or theft, and natural disasters.

- **Medical payments insurance**   This covers medical expenses for injuries. This coverage guarantees immediate medical payments for you, your passengers, and other parties, regardless of who is at fault. It also covers you and members of your household in any accident involving an automobile, whether you are on foot, on a bicycle, or in someone else's car.

- **Uninsured motorist insurance**   This coverage protects you if you are injured in an accident with others who do not carry liability insurance.

- **Extra coverage insurance**   This covers expenses such as towing, labor, and temporary replacement vehicles. These are generally defined as add-ons or endorsements to your policy.

> **fyi**
>
> Many drivers obtain only the minimum insurance requirements of their state, but others add on collision and comprehensive insurance to their policy. In some cases, collision and comprehensive insurance are required. This might be true for financed cars.

activity   **Auto Insurance Premiums**

Answer the questions.

1. A car owner pays an auto insurance premium of $72 per month. She wants to add additional coverage that will increase her premium to $85 per month. By how much will her insurance cost increase annually?

_____

2. The additional coverage protects the car owner against the expense of towing her vehicle when it breaks down. If towing costs $85 and the repair costs $120, does she still save money by having the extra coverage? If so, how much?

_____

Gas Costs

One of the greatest costs associated with driving is the cost of gasoline. Estimating your gasoline expenses depends on several factors.

key words

gas mileage

Price of Gasoline

The price of gasoline is the amount you pay per gallon of gasoline. This amount can fluctuate with international events as well as with seasonal demand.

Gas Mileage

A car's **gas mileage** is the average number of miles it can travel on one gallon of gasoline. Generally, larger cars do not travel as far on a gallon of gasoline as smaller cars.

Distance

The average distance you drive is an important consideration in determining how much gas you will need. To determine the average distance you drive, keep track of how many miles you drive in a week. Do this for several weeks to obtain a realistic average.

To estimate gas expenses, multiply the average number of miles driven by the length of time (such as weeks or months). Then divide by the gas mileage of the car and multiply by the average price of a gallon of gas.

activity | **Calculating Gas Expenses**
Answer the questions below.

1. Diego drives an average of 250 miles per week. His car gets 24 miles to the gallon. If gas costs an average of $2.50 per gallon, about how much can Diego expect to spend on gasoline each month? (Assume there are 4 weeks in a month.)

_____

2. Susan drives an average of 500 miles per week. Her car gets 20 miles to the gallon. If gas costs an average of $2.20 per gallon, about how much can Susan expect to spend on gasoline each month? (Assume there are 4 weeks in a month.)

_____

3. Mya drives an average of 400 miles per week. Her car gets 26 miles to the gallon. If gas costs an average of $2.80 per gallon, about how much can Mya expect to spend on gasoline in a year?

_____

4. Giuseppe drives an average of 300 miles per week. His car gets 18 miles to the gallon. If gas costs an average of $2.10 per gallon, about how much can Giuseppe expect to spend on gasoline in a year?

_____

Name _____ Date _____

Selling a Vehicle

At some point, you may want to sell your car. To get the most out of your sale, you need to do a little homework.

Asking Price

The first thing you should do is research to find a reasonable price for your car. Look through advertisements for comparable vehicles as well as documents, such as the Kelley Blue Book. This is a book that estimates the current value of a vehicle. As you do this, keep in mind the mileage on the car and its condition. Don't forget to consider any special features the car has or any improvements you have made to it.

Location

The next thing you need to do is decide where you are going to sell your car. You might hang a sign on it, you might put an ad in the newspaper, or you might even describe it on an Internet Web site. Be sure to take into account any costs associated with these options.

Show Off Your Car

Before you head out with your car, make sure it is detailed. A clean, shiny car will attract more attention than a dull, dirty car. If you use a sign, you may want to park your car in a place where many people will see it.

Negotiating

You may want to build a little "cushion" into the asking price of your car. This will allow you to drop the price a little for a buyer who wants to negotiate, yet still receive the amount you were looking for. Be clear with the buyer about how you expect payment. For example, will you accept cash only, or will you accept a check or cashier's check? Write down any terms of the agreement. Indicate whether you will pay for repairs for a limited time or whether the car is sold "as is."

Legal Requirements

Make sure you know the legal requirements in your state regarding any documents that need to be provided. The Certificate of Title will need to be transferred, but some states also require inspection certificates and other documents.

 Selling a Car

Complete the task below.

Dominick wants to sell his car for the Kelley Blue Book value of $10,500. Dominick spends $50 on products to detail the car and $30 to advertise the sale of the car. He asks $11,000 for the car and sells the car for $10,000.

1. What is the difference between the asking price and the selling price of the car? _____

2. Compare the overall cost of selling the car with the price at which the car is sold. _____

Chapter 6 Review
Vocabulary

Use the words from the list to complete the sentences.

asking
collision
comprehensive
lease
mileage
warranty

1. The _____ price is the amount you advertise when selling your car.

2. When you _____ a car, you make fixed payments on only a portion of a vehicle.

3. _____ auto insurance covers damage to your own vehicle incurred in an accident.

4. _____ auto insurance covers fire damage, break-ins, vandalism, and natural disasters.

5. Gas _____ is the number of miles a car can travel on one gallon of gas.

6. A(n) _____ is a promise to repair problems with the car within a certain period of time.

Comparing Auto Insurance

7. Write a paragraph comparing and contrasting the following types of auto insurance: collision, uninsured motorist, add-ons, medical payment insurance, comprehensive, general liability.

_____

_____

_____

_____

_____

_____

Extension Activity

Obtain two or three newspaper advertisements for automobiles. Compare the prices of the same model new and used. Then look for financing options offered by various companies. Note the length and terms of the offers.

Wants vs. Needs

key words

need
want

You see a beautiful new sports car driving down the street. You say you need that car. In actuality, you don't really *need* the car, but you do *want* it. In order to keep your finances in order, you need to distinguish between wants and needs.

A **need** is something that is essential. You must have it in order to survive. Food is an example of a need. Although you can go for periods of time without food, you eventually have to eat.

A **want** is something that is not a necessity. It may be something that will enhance the quality of your life, but it is something you can live without. A want is something you would like to have. An example of a want is music. While you might enjoy listening to music and it improves the quality of your life, you could survive without music.

Sometimes different versions of the same item can be either a want or a need. For example, you might need a car to get to work, but you don't need a sports car. You might need somewhere to live, but you don't need to live in a mansion.

activity | **Distinguishing Wants from Needs**

Write *W* next to the wants and *N* next to the needs.

1. A stereo system _____

2. A television _____

3. Water to drink _____

4. A place to live _____

5. Prescription medicine _____

6. A skateboard _____

7. A coat in winter _____

8. A pair of shoes _____

9. A pair of eyeglasses _____

10. A bowl of ice cream _____

Establishing a Budget

In order to set aside funds for unexpected needs, save for retirement, and meet your daily needs, you need to establish a budget. A **budget** is a plan for spending and saving money.

A budget has two parts. Money that comes in is income. Money that goes out is an expense. Income is made up of money that comes from working, gifts, allowances, and other sources. Expenses consist of such costs as rent or mortgage, insurance, car payments, food, gas, clothing, and savings.

You need to plan a budget so that your income is greater than your expenses. You cannot simply sit down and plan a budget in a few minutes. Instead, you need to take time to get an idea of what you really spend on various things.

1. To get started, keep track of all of the money coming in and going out for a few months.

2. Once you have a realistic idea, determine how much money you will receive the next month.

3. Estimate what expenses you will absolutely have to pay during the month. These will include such costs as rent, food, utilities, and other necessities of life.

4. Add up your expenses. If the total is less than your income, great! You can add some optional expenses into your budget, such as items you may want. If not, you need to ask yourself some questions.

Are there any expenses that are wants instead of needs? Can you simplify any expenses so that they cost less? If you cannot lower your expenses, you must determine if you can increase your income. Can you work more hours? Perhaps you need to consider getting an additional job or changing your job. If you cannot lower your expenses so they are below your income, you will soon find yourself in debt.

---

key words

budget

---

tip

A budget will need to change over time as income and expenses change. Be sure to update your budget frequently.

Name _____   Date _____

activity **Planning a Monthly Budget**
Follow the steps to plan a budget.

Step 1   Identify the sources of your income and the amount of each.

INCOME

_____   _____

_____   _____

_____   _____

Total Monthly Income   _____

Step 2   Identify your necessary expenses and how much each costs.
Some possible expenses are listed for you.

EXPENSES

electricity   _____

insurance   _____

food   _____

telephone   _____

_____   _____

_____   _____

_____   _____

_____   _____

_____   _____

_____   _____

Total Monthly Expenses   _____

Step 3   Subtract your total expenses from your total income.

Total Income   _____

Total Expenses   – _____

Savings/Debt   _____

Step 4 If your budget resulted in debt, go back through to see if there are expenses you can eliminate or lower. Make any corrections and find your new total expenses. _____ Repeat Step 3. Go through your budget until you no longer end up in debt.

REVISED EXPENSES _____

If your budget resulted in savings, you can add optional expenses into your budget. Add any wants that you would like to include in your budget.

    WANTS

    _____   _____

    _____   _____

    _____   _____

    Total Wants   _____

Add the Total Wants to the Total Expenses.

        Total Expenses + Total Wants = _____

Then repeat Step 3 with this new total. Make sure that you still have savings. If not, you'll need to drop some of your wants out of the budget.

Step 5 Determine how much money you can save each month.

        Total Savings _____

Step 6 Calculate your annual savings if you stay on budget.

        Total Monthly Savings × 12 = _____

Determining Net Worth

You can get an idea of your financial position by determining your net worth. Basically, your **net worth** is the difference between the things you own (assets) and the things you owe (liabilities). Your net worth gives you a snapshot of your current financial situation. Knowing your net worth can help you make financial plans for the future.

To calculate your net worth, begin by listing everything of value that you own. These are your assets. Consider all of the following:

- cash and cash equivalents, such as certificates of deposit, money market accounts, and bank accounts
- investments, such as stocks, bonds, mutual funds, and savings bonds
- retirement funds, such as 401(k) plans, IRAs, and company pension plans
- real estate, including your home, if you own it, and any other real estate or personal property, such as boats, cars, RVs, and planes
- household goods, such as furnishings, jewelry, furs, collectibles, and antiques

Next list any amounts that you owe. These are your liabilities. Consider all of the following:

- loans, such as a mortgage, student loan, bank loans, or car loans
- credit card balances
- taxes owed, such as real estate taxes or income taxes
- any miscellaneous amounts that you owe

The next step is to subtract the total liabilities from the total assets. If you have more assets than liabilities, you have a positive net worth. That's good. If you have more liabilities than assets, you have a negative net worth. That's not quite so good, but it is something you need to know.

Name _____ Date _____

Determining Net Worth

Fill in your assets and liabilities in the chart below. Use it to determine your net worth.

ASSETS		LIABILITIES	
Stocks		Mortgage(s)	
Bonds		Home-equity Loans	
Cash		Student Loan	
Retirement Accounts		Car Loan	
Value of Primary Residence		Credit Cards	
Furniture, Collectibles, Possessions		Other	
Other		Total Debts	
Total Assets			

Net Worth = Total Assets – Total Liabilities

[ ] = [ ] – [ ]

Bankruptcy

Sometimes people simply cannot develop a positive net worth. Their debts continue to outweigh their assets to the point that they can no longer pay the bills. **Bankruptcy** is a legal proceeding that serves as a last resort to give people who cannot pay their bills protection from creditors.

There are different forms of bankruptcy.

key words

bankruptcy

Chapter 7 Bankruptcy

This type of bankruptcy is usually filed by individuals or businesses that want a fresh financial start. For an individual, the court declares that person unable to pay debts. Almost all debts are then declared void. Some federal debts, such as student loans, are not affected.

Laws prevent people from declaring bankruptcy just to avoid paying their bills. A person filing Chapter 7 must prove that his or her income is not sufficient to meet debts. That person also risks losing any assets that remain because many assets are sold to pay debts.

Chapter 13 Bankruptcy

This type of bankruptcy is filed by individuals who own many assets but find that their income is not enough to meet the high cost of retaining the assets. In this form, the debt is restructured or reduced so that the people can keep their assets but pay for them in a more reasonable schedule. Payments ordered by the court must be paid on time if the person hopes to keep the assets.

An individual's credit score suffers as a result of a bankruptcy. The bankruptcy remains on the credit report for 10 years. It can make it difficult to get approved for loans and credit cards.

fyi

The release from debt given at the end of bankruptcy proceedings is called a discharge.

Chapter 11 Bankruptcy

This type of bankruptcy is used by larger businesses. It resembles Chapter 13 bankruptcy, but with additional restrictions.

Chapter 7 Review
Vocabulary

Write the term or phrase described by the clue on each line. Choose from the list below.

want   net worth
expense   bankruptcy
liability   income
asset   need

1. _____ Something you own

2. _____ A legal proceeding that gives people who cannot pay their bills protection from creditors

3. _____ Money that is taken into a household

4. _____ Something you must have to survive

5. _____ Money that is paid out of a household

6. _____ The difference between assets and liabilities

7. _____ Something you owe

8. _____ Something you would like to have

Comprehension

Circle the letter of the best answer for the questions below.

9. Which of these is a want?
   a. toothpaste
   b. swimming pool
   c. mailbox

10. Which of these is a need?
   a. a hearing aid
   b. a leather jacket
   c. ice cream

11. Which of these is an asset?
   a. certificate of deposit
   b. car loan
   c. mortgage

12. Which of these is a liability?
   a. bond
   b. credit card debt
   c. IRA

Extension Activity

Businesses must establish annual budgets just as individuals do. The operating business of a publicly owned company is available to review. Many communities and churches also release their budgets. Research the budget of a company or organization. Identify the income and the expenses.

Glossary

1040A a shortened version of the 1040 tax form that taxpayers can use if they do not qualify for the 1040EZ but do not need to complete the full 1040 (p. 70)

1040EZ a shortened version of the 1040 tax form that single and married filing jointly taxpayers can use if they earn less than $100,000, have no dependents, and do not itemize deductions (p. 67)

401K a retirement plan set up by an employer through an investment company, insurance company, or bank in which an employee can contribute a certain percentage of every paycheck up to a limit without paying taxes on it (p. 59)

adjustable-rate mortgage (ARM) a type of home loan in which the interest rate changes to reflect changes in the credit market (p. 39)

ad-valorem the description of a tax that is based on the value of something, such as real estate or personal property (p. 42)

annual percentage rate (APR) the interest rate based on simple interest for a 12-month period (p. 20)

ATM an acronym for *a*utomatic *t*eller *m*achine (p. 9)

balance the amount of money in a bank account at a given time (p. 15)

bankruptcy a legal proceeding that serves as a last resort to give people who cannot pay their bills protection from creditors (p. 90)

bond an agreement by an organization to borrow money that will be repaid at a later date in addition to specified interest that will be paid throughout the life of the loan (p. 53)

budget a plan for spending and saving money (p. 85)

certificate of deposit a type of savings certificate in which an individual deposits a certain amount of money with a bank for a fixed period, during which time the person is guaranteed a locked interest rate (p. 49)

check a document given to a person or business, which contains information directing the bank to take money out of the check writer's account and transfer it to that person or business (p. 12)

checking account a type of bank account into which you deposit money that you can spend using checks instead of cash (p. 12)

closing costs fees charged by companies and government offices that process the loan and the sale of a property (p. 36)

collateral property offered in the event that a loan is not paid back (p. 26)

compound interest interest calculated at regular intervals (p. 11)

credit card a card that allows an individual to pay for merchandise or services by borrowing against a line of credit (p. 20)

credit report a summary of an individual's financial history that includes such information as whether the person pays bills on time, how much money the person has in bank accounts, and how much money the person owes (p. 22)

credit score a number that represents a measure of a person's credit risk (p. 23)

debit card a type of ATM card that can be used to deposit or withdraw money as well as to make purchases for which the amount is immediately deducted from an account (p. 9)

deposit an amount added to a bank account (p. 7)

direct deposit an amount that is transferred electronically from an employer to an employee's bank account (p. 7)

down payment an amount paid up front when a home or other large item is purchased (p. 35)

finance charge the interest charged on the money owed to a credit card company (p. 20)

fixed-rate mortgage a type of home loan in which the borrower is charged a certain percentage of the loan as interest to the lender; the monthly payment remains the same over the life of the loan (p. 37)

gas mileage the average number of miles a vehicle can travel on one gallon of gasoline (p. 81)

grace period the length of time from when a purchase is made to when the company begins charging interest on that purchase (p. 20)

homeowner's insurance   an insurance policy that protects an individual's home, possessions, and family in the event of unexpected misfortunes (p. 40)

income tax   a tax levied on any money a person earns (p. 61)

initial public offering (IPO)   the first public offering in which a company sells stock (p. 52)

insufficient funds   a situation in which a check is not processed because there is not enough money in the account to pay it (p. 15)

interest   the money earned by using a bank account (p. 10)

IRA   an Individual Retirement Account that can be set up by an individual to save for retirement while taking advantage of tax breaks (p. 59)

itemized deductions   certain personal expenses that are allowed as deductions from the adjusted gross income (p. 73)

lease   a legal contract that defines a relationship between the owner of a rental unit, called the lessor, and the renter, called the lessee (p. 29)

loan   a sum of money lent to a borrower at some interest rate (p. 25)

minimum payment   the lowest amount that an individual is required to pay on credit card debt (p. 20)

money market   a vehicle through which large institutions and governments manage their short-term cash needs (p. 57)

mortgage   a loan secured to pay the difference between the asking price of a home and the down payment (p. 35)

mutual fund   a group of investors who work through a fund manager to purchase a portfolio of stocks or bonds; shares of the mutual funds can be purchased by individuals as investments (p. 55)

need   something that is essential to a person's survival (p. 84)

net worth   the difference between a person's assets and liabilities (p. 88)

pension   a plan set up by an employer to help employees save for retirement (p. 59)

PIN   an acronym for *p*ersonal *i*dentification *n*umber; a PIN is used to access an individual account (p. 9)

principal   the amount of money deposited or borrowed (p. 10)

property tax   a fee that the owner of a property pays on the value of the property (p. 42)

reconcile   to match your records describing a bank account balance to the records on file at the bank (p. 18)

register   a table used to calculate the balance in a bank account (p. 15)

renter's insurance   an insurance policy that can protect a renter's personal property against fire, theft, or vandalism as well as provide liability coverage in the event of a lawsuit (p. 34)

savings account   a bank account that earns money while protecting the money (p. 7)

simple interest   interest calculated once throughout the life of a loan or deposit; calculated by multiplying the principal by the interest rate by the term (p. 10)

standard deduction   a fixed dollar amount that depends on an individual's filing status; the amount is subtracted from gross earnings before calculating the tax owed (p. 62)

stock   a part, or share, of ownership in a company (p. 51)

term   the length of time determined for paying back a loan (p. 25)

utilities   services that are utilized by individuals, such as gas, electricity, water, and sewers (p. 43)

W-2   a tax form on which an employer reports wages, tax withholdings, and other vital information (p. 65)

want   a nonessential item that a person would like to have (p. 84)

warranty   a promise from a car dealer or manufacturer to an individual who purchases a car to repair problems with the car within a certain period of time or a certain number of miles (p. 77)

withdrawal   an amount removed from a bank account (p. 8)

Glossary
Financial Math 2, SV 9781419034381

Answer Key

pp. 5–6, Assessment

1. B	11. B
2. C	12. C
3. C	13. B
4. B	14. A
5. A	15. D
6. A	16. B
7. D	17. D
8. A	18. B
9. D	19. C
10. D	20. A

p. 7

1. Local Savings Bank
2. $56.12
3. $144.98
4. 2170121
5. $201.10

p. 8

1. April 15, 2008
2. Ninety-three dollars and fifty cents
3. 817212
4. Working Bank
5. 468151242

p. 9

1. $68.26
2. $88.12

p. 10

1. $20, $120
2. $52.50, $1,052.50
3. $46,200, $74,200
4. $405,000, $585,000

p. 11

1. $10,600.00
2. $10,613.64
3. $10,616.78
4. $10,618.31
5. No, there is not a major difference. It amounts to $18.31.
6. $11,255.09

p. 14

Students should fill in all of the information provided in the proper places and then sign the checks.

p. 15

1. $1,295.82
2. $1,192.67
3. $50
4. $153.15

p. 16

NUMBER/Code	DATE	TRANSACTION DESCRIPTION	PAYMENT/DEBIT		FEE	DEPOSIT/CREDIT		BALANCE $1,295.82	
191	11/10	Current News Co.	24	30				1,168	37
Debit	11/11	All About Food	68	51				1,099	86
Deposit	11/14	Paycheck/Quick Delivery Service				892	78	1,992	64
192	11/15	Speedy Cars	252	25				1,740	39

Ending balance = $1,740.39

p. 18

Students should insert check 517, which is missing from the register. They should then subtract the last two entries because they occurred after the bank statement was prepared.

p. 19, Chapter 1 Review

1. savings
2. interest
3. check
4. balance
5. deposit
6. insufficient funds
7. debit
8. principal
9. withdrawal
10. PIN
11. Answers may vary. Students may suggest that carrying a card is safer than carrying cash that can be lost or stolen. Another advantage is that it enables the user to bank 24 hours a day, seven days a week.
12. Compound interest is determined at specific intervals and added to the principal. The original principal plus the interest earned then earns interest during the next interval. Simple interest is calculated once through the life of a deposit or loan.
13. The routing number identifies the bank. The account number identifies a person's account within a specific bank.
14. When you reconcile your checkbook register, you make sure your records match the bank's records.

p. 21

1. $150
2. $2.25
3. $50
4. $75
5. $39.17 (assume the daily average balance is $250)

p. 23

1. John Doe
2. March 4, 2008
3. AMEX (American Express)
4. $978
5. December, 1999
6. PRM VISA, NATIONS BANK, AM CITIBANK, and GE CAPITAL
7. Insufficient funds

p. 25

1. $5,000
2. 8.2%
3. 5 years

p. 26

$55,000

pp. 27–28, Chapter 2 Review

1. credit card
2. grace period
3. minimum payment
4. balance
5. finance charge
6. loan
7. credit report
8. credit score
9. APR
10. installment
11. line of credit
12. principal
13. term
14. Answers will vary. Using a credit card will enable a person to purchase items without having to carry around a lot of cash. It also allows the person to hold on to the money for the length of the grace period, during which time it may earn interest in a bank account.

15. Check that students have completed the form. Be sure to destroy the completed forms or distribute them to students so that personal information is not lost.

p. 30

1. $25,000
2. $19,440
3. $1,110
4. $15,350
5. $28,000
6. $950 per month

p. 32

1. May 15, 2008
2. Rita Renter
3. the fifth day of the month
4. $1,100
5. $10 per day
6. tenant
7. landlord
8. $1,100
9. June 1, 2008
10. 12 months
11. J and L Enterprises
12. May 31, 2009
13. check
14. gas, water, and heat
15. none

p. 34

Renter A pays $140 for the policy plus $625 for a new stereo. Renter A receives an insurance payment of $125.

Renter B pays $180 for the policy plus $625 for a new stereo. Renter B receives an insurance payment of $625.

Renter B has a lower total expense.

p. 35

1. $48,000
2. $46,250
3. Annual PMI: $450
   Monthly PMI: $37.50
4. Annual PMI: $1,020
   Monthly PMI: $85.00

p. 36

1. $6,000
2. $3,500
3. $300,000
4. $14,625
5. You would not pay interest on the closing costs. If closing costs were rolled into your mortgage, you would end up paying a lot more money in the long run.

Answer Key
Financial Math 2, SV 9781419034381

p. 38
1. $269,798
2. $125,109
3. about 1.6 times
4. Point costs $1,250; interest is reduced by $31,886

p. 39
1. 9%
2. 3 years

p. 41
1. c
2. Students should develop a complete list of possessions and suggested values.

p. 42
1. $1,000
2. $2,500

p. 43
1. $2.188
2. $43.62
3. $0.15
4. Q1; Q3
5. November through May

p. 44
1. 32 cents
2. 79 cents
3. $2.12
4. 59 cents
5. $1.32
6. 53 cents
7. $3.97

p. 45
1. 123-45-0
2. 79564
3. 7/12/08
4. 16.41 therms
5. $2.95
6. 7/30/08
7. $56.35

pp. 47–48, Chapter 3 Review
Across
2. therm
5. PMI
6. watts
7. replacement
9. down
11. insurance
13. closing
14. adjustable
Down
1. property
3. utilities
4. fixed
8. mortgage
10. deductible
12. actual
15. When a renter pays a fixed lease, he or she pays a flat fee every month. The renter must pay utilities

and other expenses related to the unit separately. In a gross lease, the renter also pays a flat fee. However, the landlord pays utilities and expenses out of that fee.
16. A security deposit protects the landlord from loss in case the renter causes damage to the rental unit. The landlord is entitled to hold fees from the deposit to pay for repairs to the unit.
17. Answers will vary. A renter has the right to live in a safe place that meets local building and health codes. A renter is guaranteed the rent stated in the lease until the end of the contract. A renter must be informed of any change in management, ownership, or other use of the property.
18. Answers will vary. A renter must provide true and accurate information in the application. A renter must pay the rent on time without having to be reminded by the landlord. A renter must keep the rental unit in good condition.
19. The landlord's homeowner's insurance protects the landlord and the building. Renter's insurance would protect the renter's possessions. It would also protect the renter from damages or injuries that occur at the rental unit.
20. A down payment is money paid up front for the purchase of a home. The down payment cannot be borrowed. The mortgage is a loan for the difference between the price of the home and the down payment.
21. PMI protects the lender in the event that the borrower defaults on the loan.
22. Discount points reduce the interest rate charged on the mortgage. Interest can add up substantially

over the course of a loan, so decreasing the interest rate can save thousands of dollars in the long run.
23. A 30-year term loan has lower payments over a longer period of time. The borrower usually has the option to prepay the principal early. A 15-year term loan has a higher payment for a shorter period of time. It also generally has a lower interest rate.
24. The deductible is the amount the policyholder must pay before receiving benefits. The higher the deductible, the lower the risk assumed by the insurance company, so the lower the premiums can be.

p. 50
1. 0.01%
2. 0.15%
3. 0.14%
4. 0.05%

p. 51
1. $25
2. 20 shares

p. 52
1. $1,525
2. $5,100
3. $195
4. $800

p. 54
1. 7.5%
2. 10%
3. 6.5%
4. 5.0%

p. 55
1. $160
2. 125 shares
3. $500
4. $560

p. 57
1. 1.65%
2. 1.65%
3. 3.15%
4. 4.25%

p. 58
1. about 23%
2. another 47%, or $1,974

p. 59
1. $36
2. $18
3. $54

p. 60, Chapter 4 Review
1. E
2. D
3. F
4. I
5. H
6. J
7. C
8. A
9. G
10. B

p. 61
1. YES
2. NO
3. YES
4. NO
5. YES

p. 62
1. $5,150
2. $7,550
3. $5,150
4. $10,300

p. 63
1. $11,834
2. $13,791
3. $14,414
4. $12,501

p. 64
$43,341.50

p. 66
1. $12,929.79
2. $856.11
3. $199.45
4. 0
5. California
6. Freezy Ice Cream Co.

p. 68
Check to see that students complete the form properly.

p. 70
Check to see that students complete the form properly.

p. 74
Check to see that students complete the form properly.

p. 76, Chapter 5 Review
1. April 15
2. Their gross income is below a certain amount stipulated by the IRS.
3. It is a fixed dollar amount that is subtracted from gross income before calculating taxes. It depends on the filing status.
4. Wages and tax withholdings are reported along with personal

information about an employee.

5. a, c, d, f

6. Answers will vary but may include medical expenses, property taxes, and mortgage interest.

p. 77

Answers will vary. The new car has a higher overall cost of $15,320 including the annual insurance premium and registration. The used car has a lower overall cost of $7,520. The new car comes with a warranty, whereas the used car does not. The used car may require repairs that are not covered by any warranty.

p. 78

1. $7,458
2. $3,414.80
3. $2,506.60

p. 79

Answers will vary. The lease payment is much lower than the loan payments at either 0% or 6% interest. Everything else is the same except for the residual value of the lease. This is the value of the car at the end of the lease. If a person were to purchase the car at the end of the lease, he or she would spend considerably more than with either of the loans.

p. 80

1. It increases by $156.
2. Yes, she saves $49.

p. 81

1. $104.17
2. $220
3. $2,240
4. $1,820

p. 82

1. $1,000 less than the asking price of the car
2. Dominick wants $10,500 for the car. He sells it for $500 less than he wanted. In addition, he spent $80 in selling the car.

p. 83, Chapter 6 Review

1. asking
2. lease
3. Collision
4. Comprehensive
5. mileage
6. warranty

7. Answers will vary. All types of auto insurance protect the owner of a car. Collision covers damage to the vehicle incurred in an accident. General liability covers damages caused to other people's property or to the people themselves. Comprehensive covers fire damage, break-ins, vandalism, and natural disasters. Medical payment insurance covers medical expenses for injuries. Uninsured motorist protects you if you are injured in an accident with others who do not carry liability insurance. Add-ons cover such expenses as towing, labor, and temporary replacement vehicles.

p. 84

1. W
2. W
3. N
4. N
5. N
6. W
7. N
8. N
9. N
10. W

pp. 86–87

Check that students have completed their budgets to result in savings.

p. 89

Check to see that students have determined their net worth.

p. 91, Chapter 7 Review

1. Asset
2. Bankruptcy
3. Income
4. Need
5. Expense
6. Net worth
7. Liability
8. Want
9. b
10. a
11. a
12. b

CPSIA information can be obtained
at www.ICGtesting.com
Printed in the USA
BVHW060945250821
615137BV00009B/554